Melven's Bookshop

of

Inverness

Oct. 1968.

THE
ROYAL DEESIDE
LINE

UNIFORM WITH THIS BOOK

The Callander & Oban Railway, by John Thomas
The Cambrian Railways, Volume 1: 1852-1888 and *Volume 2: 1888-1967,* by Rex Christiansen and R. W. Miller
The Cavan & Leitrim Railway, by Patrick J. Flanagan
The Great North of Scotland Railway, by H. A. Vallance
The Highland Railway, by H. A. Vallance
A History of the Narrow-gauge Railways of North East Ireland, by Edward M. Patterson: *Part One—The Ballycastle Railway. Part Two—The Ballymena Lines*
A History of the Narrow-gauge Railways of North West Ireland, by Edward M. Patterson: *Part One—The County Donegal Railways. Second Edition. Part Two—The Londonderry & Lough Swilly Railway*
A History of the Railways of the Forest of Dean, by H. W. Paar: *Part One—The Severn & Wye Railway. Part Two—The Great Western Railway in Dean*
The London & South Western Railway, Volume 1, by R. A. Williams
The Lynton & Barnstaple Railway, by G. A. Brown, J. D. C. A. Prideaux and H. G. Radcliffe
The Midland & South Western Junction Railway, by Colin G. Maggs
The Somerset & Dorset Railway, by Robin Atthill and O. S. Nock
The West Highland Railway, by John Thomas

IN PREPARATION

The Lancashire & Yorkshire Railway, by John Marshall (two volumes)
The London & North Western Railway, by M. C. Reed (three volumes)
The London & South Western Railway, Volumes 2 and 3, by R. A. Williams
The Midland & Great Northern Joint Railway, by A. J. Wrottesley
The North Staffordshire Railway, by Rex Christiansen and R. W. Miller
The Ravenglass & Eskdale Railway, by W. J. K. Davies

Passing the 'Shakin' Briggie' at Cults, about 1865; a down train hauled by one of the Deeside Railway Company's Hawthorn 0—4—2 locomotives, No 4

THE
ROYAL DEESIDE
LINE

by

A. D. FARR

DAVID & CHARLES : NEWTON ABBOT

7153 4273 8

TO DAVID
—who is growing up
within sight of the line,
but will only know it
through this book.

Printed in Great Britain
by Bristol Typesetting Company Limited
for David & Charles (Holdings) Limited
South Devon House Newton Abbot Devon

Contents

APPENDIXES

List of Illustrations

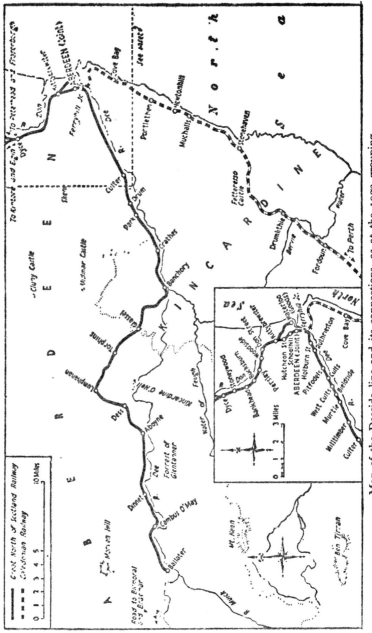

Map of the Deeside line and its connections, as at the 1923 grouping

The scenery's grand, the air, oh! it's charming,
  Deeside being famed for excellent farming;
The mountains stupendous, and sweet heathery plains—
  Travelling's pleasant, there's well arranged trains.
                    (from an advertisement published in 1866
                    by Samuel Martin, Hatter, of Aberdeen)

CHAPTER 1

In the Beginning

Of all the branch lines in Britain probably none is so well known —even if only by name—as that which ran along Royal Deeside. Through its natural beauty and its connections with the Royal family, Deeside has become one of Scotland's best-known tourist centres and its beauty has become proverbial throughout the kingdom. The railway that followed the course of the Dee provided a journey of great scenic attraction through the lowlands of Aberdeenshire to the gateway of the old highland kingdom of Mar.

For centuries the Dee valley has been an important route linking the inhospitable mountains with the coast. Economically, it has been valuable also as one of the best salmon rivers in the country. Its waters are remarkably clear everywhere, and the valleys and glens that give birth to its tributaries contain some of the finest scenery that the Highlands—indeed the whole of Britain —has to offer. The combination of these factors with the dry, bracing climate and pure clear air would in any case have made the area a favourite goal for tourists and holidaymakers; the presence of the royal estates at Balmoral has clinched the matter and attracted a considerable tourist trade to the district.

The estate of Balmoral, with the old castle, was first leased in 1848, and in 1851 purchased, by the Prince Consort from the trustees of the Earl of Fife for £31,500. The Prince Consort gave Balmoral to the Queen, who in turn left her 'Highland home' as a holiday residence for subsequent sovereigns. The regular presence on Deeside of Her Majesty undoubtedly gave a considerable impetus to the expansion of communications along the valley and earned for it the *sobriquet* Royal Deeside. From the opening of the railway in 1853 until its closure at the end of 1966 five generations of reigning monarchs regularly travelled to and from their Scottish home via the Deeside line but, alas, the coming of modern roads and the ever-spreading influence of the internal combustion engine have finally resulted in the closure of this well-loved railway. Falling traffic receipts—both passenger and freight—together with ever-rising costs, failures to economise and re-organise, and the modern trend to streamline British railway facilities into a largely main-line system, have brought the line under the 'Beeching axe'.

Now that the Deeside trains no longer run it is possible to look back and survey the line's colourful past. The first complete railway line in Aberdeenshire, a regular carrier of two reigning queens and four kings of Great Britain (as well as, on occasion, the Czar of all the Russias and other assorted foreign royalty) and the one-time owner (so tradition says) of a locomotive painted in the Royal Stuart tartan, the Deeside line finally died aged 113 years, three months and twenty-two days, mourned by many. It was in many respects a truly unique line, and indeed this word will be found frequently in the text as describing many facets of the line throughout its history. It has left behind a fascinating story that is itself the line's best obituary and memorial.

FIRST PROPOSALS

The first suggestions for a railway along the Dee valley that achieved any concrete form were made in 1845. Following a meeting on 2 September of that year, a prospectus was issued for a 'Deeside Railway'.

The Board of the new company was to consist of Thomas Blaikie (who as well as being Lord Provost of Aberdeen was also Chairman of the Great North) as Chairman, together with the directors of the Aberdeen Railway Company and the directors of the Great North of Scotland Railway. Alexander Gibb was to be the Engineer. The original capital was to consist of £100,000 (issued in 2,000 shares of £50 each) which was to cover the estimated cost of £95,009 19s 1d for constructing a single line along the north side of the river as far as Banchory.

After the manner of its kind, the prospectus was eloquent and extensive in detailing the advantages of its proposals. It was stated that the result of an enquiry into the potential traffic 'has exceeded all expectations'. Suggestions were made for improving the fords and ferries over the Dee, and building a new bridge over it (nearly opposite Durris House) to help feed the proposed line.

The distance to Banchory by the proposed route was seventeen miles, one mile less than the turnpike road, and a ruling gradient of

1 in 278 was envisaged. The author then gave his artistic bent temporary control.

> It will readily be believed by those who are acquainted with the beautiful scenery and superior climate of Deeside, that far more than the usual increase of Passenger Traffic might be assumed for a Railway which connects the Port and populous City of Aberdeen —having great Trunk Lines of Railway both to the south and north—with the upper district of Deeside, which is known to be the principal resort of the inhabitants of the adjacent towns, and of Tourists from all parts of the kingdom.

In passing, it may be noted that, on the date of the prospectus first appearing, the afore-mentioned 'great Trunk Lines of Railway both to the south and north' consisted of an embryo Parliamentary Bill to the north and a two-month old Act to the south. Trains did not actually begin to run until 1850 to and from the south, and until 1854 to the north—a year after the Deeside Railway itself eventually opened. Viewed from the 1960s, the financial prospects foreseen by the promoters cannot but engender a feeling of awe for their magnificent and masterly simplicity.

> It is impossible to estimate the increase, either of Passenger or Goods Traffic accurately; but taking the amount presently paid for tolls and carriages on the two turnpike roads, as above estimated at £7,000
> and add the estimated sum paid for floating and logging wood down the river, and carriages by other roads, as above ... £2,000
> and for increase both on Passenger and Goods Traffic, say only £5,000
> the amount of traffic would be £14,000
> from which deduct working expenses £5,000
> there remains £9,000
> which will give a return of 9 per cent on the estimated amount of cost. But as it is proposed to take powers in the Bill to sell or lease the line to the Aberdeen Railway Company, so as to save expense on the moving plant and working, it is not improbable that a much larger percentage on the capital will be realised than above stated.

And to clinch the promoters' case the prospective shareholders were assured that 'the proprietors along the line are most favourable to the undertaking.'

So highly did the new project commend itself to the public that only a week after it was first announced the *Aberdeen Herald* could report '. . . that before twelve o'clock on Saturday application had been made for the whole number of shares, and speculators were busy, in the afternoon, buying up promises or expectations at a premium.' The same paper went on to comment that '. . . there is only wanting the means of cheap and speedy conveyance to

cause the whole of Deeside to be studded with villas and cottages
as thickly as the Banks of the Clyde . . . God speed the Deeside
Railway.'

So well did the public respond that a further survey was made,
and at a meeting held on 24 September it was decided that a line
should be constructed all the way to Aboyne and that the capital
should be increased to £220,000. West of Banchory the line was to
follow closely the turnpike road as far as Kincardine O'Neil,
passing over an embankment to the south of that village and then
crossing the river about half a mile further on and re-crossing it
after another mile, above the Mill of Dess. Approaching Aboyne
the line would run round the north of Aboyne Loch, crossing part
of it and finishing in Aboyne to the north of the main road.

The new total mileage was now 29¼ miles from Ferryhill with 1
in 103 as the maximum gradient. This additional section involved
rather heavier engineering works than the original plan—hence
an increase of 120 per cent in the capital to cover an increase of 70
per cent in mileage. Apart from the two bridges over the Dee there
were two lengthy and steep embankments involved in the approach
to these. Despite these complications the line was still considered
a good speculation, for a fortnight later the local press reported
that stock had been applied for to six times its amount. In due
course the proposals were incorporated into a Parliamentary Bill,
which was duly approved, and 'An Act for making a Railway from
Ferryhill near *Aberdeen* to *Aboyne* to be called the "Deeside Railway"' received Royal Assent on 16 July 1846.

Unfortunately, hopes of a 'cheap and speedy conveyance' along
Deeside were doomed to suffer a delay of some years before becoming a reality.

Although the Deeside company was well placed as regards
capital, financial problems elsewhere indirectly affected it, and on
4 September a decision was made, subsequently ratified at the first
ordinary general meeting seven days later, 'to defer proceeding
with the Works for Twelve Months or until they (the Directors)
shall receive the sanction of a General Meeting of the Shareholders'. This delay was in order that the heavy plant needed could
be obtained from the Aberdeen Railway—which would then be
nearer completion—more cheaply than elsewhere.

Unfortunately the Aberdeen company suffered delays due to the
financial crisis that followed the boom years of railway mania
before 1846—although these were not anything like as severe as
those which troubled its neighbour, the Great North of Scotland

Page 17 : THREE GENERATIONS

(1) GNS *train at Cambus O'May, about* 1910

(2) BR *standard* 4MTTs *at Torphins*

(3) *Diesel railcar by Tullich Lodge,* 1965

Page 18: THE BEGINNING

(4) *Invitation to the cutting of the first turf*
(5) *Barrow and spade used to cut the first turf at Park, 5 July 1852*

Railway—and completion of the line to a temporary station at Ferryhill was not effected until the spring of 1850.

To help expedite completion of the Aberdeen Railway, the Deeside company loaned £16,000 of its capital to that company as a debenture bond in 1847. A year later, there still being no sign of work commencing on the Deeside line, a large section of the shareholders petitioned for a dissolution of the company and a division of its assets. Fortunately there was still sufficient faith in the project to save the day. The Aberdeen Railway used its loan from the Deeside to buy up the shares from the dissident faction, thus obtaining a strong voice in the affairs of the company.

Good fortune seemed to be hovering over the Deeside project, for a year later (in 1849), a number of local people got over the post-railway mania depression and began to show a revived interest in the construction of a Deeside Railway. The Aberdeen Railway—perhaps shortsightedly in the light of subsequent happenings—promptly sold its Deeside shares to these people.

ALL CLEAR

Before any further positive steps were taken towards building the line, the ground was well prepared by Robert Notman, an Aberdeen accountant, who in March 1850 published a pamphlet in the form of an open letter to the landed proprietors of Deeside. In this he pointed out the advantages of a railway and made some carefully calculated proposals as to how this could best be effected. Basically, a single line was proposed to go only as far as Banchory in the first instance. He 'computed the expense of land, earth, and stone works, rails, chairs, and sleepers, stations, engineering, and law charges' and concluded that the line could be built for £83,500 instead of the £100,000 previously suggested.

The calculations were based on two conditions—that 'in station houses and the works generally, utility and not show shall be consulted; and, secondly, he objects to anything like extravagance in the allowances for land' (*Aberdeen Herald* 16 March 1850). This latter was a particularly apt point, for in the years of railway mania landowners had been pursuing a general policy of charging entirely exorbitant figures for the development of their property.

Notman thought that as the landowners on Deeside stood to gain most from the railway, they should give up their land at a fair agricultural price and dispense with 'intersectional and amenity damages'. Of the sixteen miles between Aberdeen and Banchory he

B

calculated that eleven miles could be obtained by feu at a low rent, and the remainder bought inexpensively.

Notman also suggested that the Aberdeen Railway should work the line 'as well as affording gratuitous, or at least very cheap, terminal accommodation'. If it was decided that the company should work the line itself the moveable plant would cost £13,200. As a final fillip to the imagination of his readers Notman pointed out that at that time, even in the depths of winter, not less than three four-horse carriages and about thirty carriers were plying on the Deeside roads. About 140,000 passengers a year and an annual dividend of at least 9½ per cent could be expected, he claimed. The local press thought his claims erred, if at all, on the modest side. The *Aberdeen Herald* waxed eloquent on the theme, referring to

> the Deeside which, besides opening up an important agricultural district, will afford to the inhabitants of Aberdeen an opportunity of breathing the fresh air in a climate milder than their own, and amongst some of the finest scenery in the world.

This was what the promoters had been saying all along. But the *Herald* pointed its homily directly at the landed proprietors to whom Notman's appeal was primarily addressed.

> In the face of so much bungling and mismanagement, the magnates of the money market will not come forward unless they find that the undertaking is liberally supported by parties locally interested, and acquainted with the circumstances.

This fine public-spirited support for the Deeside project was given added *piquance* by the report in the following week's issue of the opening of the Aberdeen Railway. The unknown reporter put a sting in the tail of his report of this event, commenting that

> to reap the full advantage of the Railway System, it must not stop at Aberdeen. If it did, the City would feel itself like a man with one arm.

A week later the Aberdeen Railway was completed (establishing through communication with London *via* Perth) on All Fools Day. If the significance of this date as an omen occurred to the supporters of the rival companies in the area, it was certainly outweighed by the obvious advantages of continuing the 'Railway System' beyond the city, both to the north and the west.

During 1850 a committee was appointed to negotiate with the landowners along the proposed route of the line and, whether or not Notman's open letter was in any way responsible, they were found to be generally willing to accept reasonable terms from the company. Matters moved slowly, but they were moving, and the general meeting on 25 November 1851 saw the beginning of the legal manoeuvres that culminated in the start of the construction.

THE ACT

Twelve days before the general meeting a notice appeared in the *Aberdeen Journal*, signed by the Chairman (John Duncan) and Vice Chairman, stating the company's intention of applying to Parliament

> for leave to bring in a Bill to alter, amend, extend, and enlarge, and to repeal some of the powers and provisions of The Deeside Railway Act, 1846, or wholly to repeal the said Act, and to make other provisions in lieu thereof.

A new survey of the route had been made by Locke and Errington, and Notman's proposals were being largely taken up. It had been ascertained that the works could be completed for a sum of £65,000, the contractors binding themselves to 'finish the Railway, and to uphold it for twelve months thereafter' at that price—a little over £4,000 a mile. Notman's hopes of the landowners being reasonable in their demands were fulfilled, and the general meeting was informed that most of the property needed would be ceded for low annual feu-duties. The directors were confident that the capital required for the total expenditure would not exceed £85,000 or £8 per share. As the company would be authorised in the proposed new Act to borrow one-third of the proposed capital, only £5 a share would need to be called up. Amidst much mutual approbation the resolutions were 'then read and agreed to'.

John Duncan had promised that time would not be lost, and this promise was faithfully kept. A Bill was introduced into Parliament and, six months later, on 28 May 1852, Royal Assent was given to:

> An Act for enabling the *Deeside* Railway Company to alter the Line and Levels of Part of their Railway, and to abandon Parts thereof; for altering the Capital of the Company, and repealing and amending the Act relating thereto; and for other purposes.

In this Act (short title—The Deeside Railway Act, 1852) the capital was given as £106,250, to consist of 10,625 shares of £10 each, of which 8s was to be the paid-up amount. There were to be six directors, and the first board consisted of:

John Blaikie	William Henderson
Patrick Davidson	Alexander John Kinloch
John Duncan	Andrew Robertson

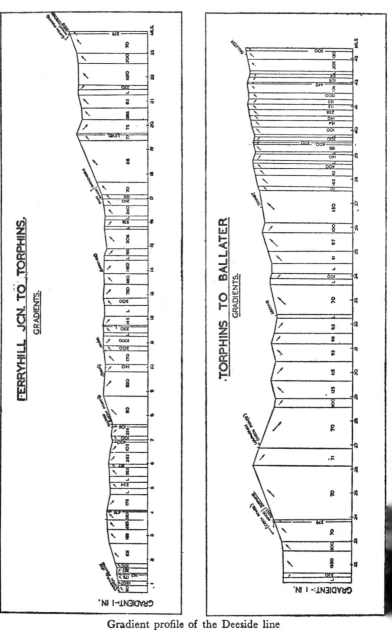

Gradient profile of the Deeside line

Coming to the line itself, the Act provided for:

> A Railway commencing at or near the Place or Point of Junction
> of the authorised Line of the *Deeside* Railway with the Line of the
> *Aberdeen Railway* . . . and terminating at or near the Free Church
> at *Banchory.*

Crest of the Deeside Railway Company

The time given for completion of the line was four years.
Finally, the Act enabled the abandonment of plans for carrying
the line beyond Banchory.

At the general meeting of 1851 the chairman had promised that,
once the new Act was obtained,

> not a day would be lost in entering into the contracts and getting
> the spade into the ground . . . Let it be distinctly known to the
> world, said Mr D, that our determination is, that the line shall go
> on, and no mistake.

In token of that pledge only five and a half weeks after the Bill
was passed into Law, on 5 July, the company got 'the spade into
the ground' and the first sod was cut.

CHAPTER 2

Guild Street to the Gairn Water

CUTTING OF THE FIRST TURF

The ceremony of cutting the first turf of the Deeside Railway was celebrated 'with the customary forms observed on such occasions' on Monday, 5 July 1852. The site selected was close to the Turnpike road, a short way above the Mains of Drum,

> and contiguous to the policies of the Mansion-house of Park, the seat of Alex Kinloch, Esq . . . A tasteful mahogany barrow and steel spade, bearing the arms and motto (" *Non Degener*") of Mr Kinloch, stood in readiness for the interesting operation to be performed by the fair lady of the manor. The weather was beautiful.

A large crowd had gathered and, at a little after one o'clock, following 'appropriate and impressive prayer' and a speech by John Duncan, Mrs Kinloch

> in a graceful manner, cut a pretty large turf, and placed it on the barrow, amidst loud cheers, which were continued when Master A. J. Kinloch, eldest son of Mr and Mrs Kinloch, immediately took hold of the barrow, and rolled it along the gangway.

After the directors had also partaken in the delights of trundling barrows of turfs more speeches were made, concluding with a toast, 'God speed the line'. After three hearty cheers for Mrs Kinloch, cake and wine was dispensed to all present and the VIP party retired to the mansion-house where they 'were entertained to a very elegant *dejeuner*'.

Construction of the line was not to be just 'cakes and wine', for the chairman had expressed the hope that the work would be completed within twelve months, 'and he trusted that before August 1853, everyone of them would be riding on the Deeside Railway'. Perhaps he had given such an early date as a spur to the contractor, but nevertheless the railway was actually opened for traffic early in the September of 1853, only fourteen months and three days after the turf-cutting ceremony.

During the writing of this book it was discovered that the barrow and spade used for the ceremony still existed and were in the possession of Mrs Kinloch's granddaughter, and these historic relics have now been presented to the Regional Museum in Aberdeen.

The contractor was Messrs Leslie & Davidson, and John Willett of Locke & Errington was the Resident Engineer. The line to be built was, from the engineering viewpoint, extremely straightforward. It was single throughout and followed a more or less straight line through fairly flat country for sixteen and three-quarter miles, with only very light earthworks.

The only piece of engineering involved that was at all out of the ordinary was the bridge over the Culter Burn. This was of five spans and was of wooden construction. Before reaching its terminus the railway had five stations and a halt. The stations were situated at Cults (3 miles from Ferryhill Junction), Murtle ($4\frac{3}{4}$ miles), Culter ($6\frac{3}{4}$ miles), Park ($10\frac{1}{8}$ miles), and Mills of Drum ($12\frac{3}{8}$ miles).

The halt was a private platform between Mills of Drum and Banchory to serve Crathes Castle. At the Aberdeen terminus the Deeside Railway shared facilities with the Aberdeen Railway's temporary station at Ferryhill Junction, while at the other end of the line a slightly larger station was built at Banchory ($16\frac{1}{8}$ miles), to the east of the town near the Free Church. The stations had been built with Robert Notman's ideas of 'utility, not show' in mind.

At Banchory there was a group of low wooden huts on the short platform serving both for waiting room and office accommodation, while close by was a separate and rather larger wooden building used as a refreshment room. The intermediate stations were less fortunate in having only a single small wooden hut on the platform—with the exception of Mills of Drum, which boasted only a box to hold the tickets.

Initially, all the stations had short platforms, which were quite insufficient to take the full length of a train. Some years later, the financial situation having improved, the wooden buildings were replaced with more substantial structures and in passing it may be noted that some of the smaller station buildings thus rebuilt (for example, Park and the later, identical, station at Crathes) contrived, although simple in design, to be extremely attractive examples of railway architecture.

The line was formally opened on 7 September 1853.

THE OPENING

Some two hundred invitation tickets were issued for the official opening,

> and by twelve o'clock a party nearly amounting to this number had assembled at the Ferryhill Station, eager to participate in the pleasures of the day. The weather was delightful. At exactly a quarter past the hour noted, the engineer shrieked out his shrill warning—the City Band cheerily struck up *Hey Johnnie Cope are ye waukin' yet*—the numerous spectators sent forth a joyous shout, and the train started on its maiden trip to Banchory.

All along the line groups of spectators had gathered to watch the apparition and, at Park,

> where the operations were commenced last year, a triumphal arch was erected, gaudily bedecked with flowers, and surmounted with the barrow and spade used by the Lady of A. J. Kinloch, Esq, in cutting the first turf.

On arrival at Banchory at one o'clock a procession proceeded to the Burnett Arms Inn, where the Provost presented a petition to the chairman 'praying that the designation of the line be changed from the "Deeside" to the "Banchory Railway" '. After this, the party then returned to the station and sat down to luncheon.

Toasts were drunk in such profusion that it is little wonder that when the company broke up three hours later there were 'a few stragglers, who seemed so captivated with the sweets of Banchory, as to have forgotten home'. With 'the snorting of the iron steed giving warning that the hour fixed for departure had arrived' the passengers boarded and the train started back for Aberdeen 'amid the loud huzzas of the spectators', and arrived back at Ferryhill a few minutes after six o'clock. The journey had taken forty-seven minutes.

The following day, Thursday the 8th, the line was opened to the public for traffic and was 'very successful in the passenger department. No fewer than 1,000 enjoyed a trip on Saturday.' Once again the local press was eloquent in extolling the merits of Deeside and its railway.

Immediately beneath this report the proprietors of the Deeside coaches announced the withdrawal of the *Prince of Wales* and the *Marquis of Huntly* coaches between Aberdeen and Banchory. The old order had begun to change.

DEESIDE RAILWAY.

OPENING OF THE LINE FOR TRAFFIC.

ON and after THURSDAY the 8th SEPTEMBER, and until further notice, Trains will leave ABERDEEN and BANCHORY at the Hours undernoted:—

Departure from Aberdeen.

Miles.	TRAINS LEAVE	1. CLASSES 1 & 3.	2. CLASSES 1 & 3.	3. CLASSES 1 & 3.
	Aberdeen ....depart	7 0 A.M.	11·0 A.M.	4·30 P.M.
3¼	Cults	7·12 ,,	11·12 ,,	4 42 ,,
4¾	Murtle	7·18 ,,	11·18 ,,	4·48 ,,
7	Culter...................	7·26 ,,	11·26 ,,	4·56 ,,
10¼	Park	7·38 ,,	11·38 ,,	5·8 ,,
12½	Mills of Drum	7·46 ,,	11·47 ,,	5·17 ,,
16¼	Banchory . ...arrive	8·0 ,,	12·0 ,,	5·30 ,,

Arrivals in Aberdeen.

Miles.	TRAINS LEAVE	1. CLASSES 1 & 3.	2. CLASSES 1 & 3.	3. CLASSES 1 & 3.
	Banchory ....depart	8·30 A.M.	1·0 P.M.	6·30 P.M.
3¾	Mills of Drum	8·44 ,,	1·13 ,,	6·43 ,,
6	Park	8·53 ,,	1·22 ,,	6·52 ,,
9¼	Culter...................	9·5 ,,	1·34 ,,	7·4 ,,
11½	Murtle	9·13 ,,	1·42 ,,	7·12 ,,
13	Cults	9·18 ,,	1·48 ,,	7·18 ,,
16¼	Aberdeen ....arrive	9·30 ,,	2·0 ,,	7·30 ,,

Announcement of the opening of the line to Banchory, 1853

CONSOLIDATION

Once the railway had been opened it soon proved its value, so much so that in the following year extra stations were provided at Milltimber (5⅝ miles from Ferryhill) and Drum (9¼ miles). In

1854 also the terminus at Aberdeen moved ⅜ mile to the north. The station shared with the Aberdeen Railway at Ferryhill had never been more than a temporary affair. Originally, the Aberdeen Railway had intended to build a station just east of Market Street, but in 1850 this plan was abandoned and powers were obtained to build the station just south of the junction of Guild Street and Market Street.

It was intended that the new station should be used jointly with the Great North of Scotland Railway, but at this time relations were becoming strained between the companies, and the Great North went off in a huff, intending to build its own terminus elsewhere. It was generally considered that the Guild Street site was cramped and too far from the city centre, but nevertheless the station was built and opened on 2 August 1854.

The Deeside Railway made good use of the move, and obtained running powers over the Aberdeen Railway's lines between Ferryhill and Guild Street, together with use of the new station. For this service the Deeside paid a fee of £700 a year for the first three years, and £1,000 a year thereafter. There was also a provision that if the Deeside's total traffic exceeded £12,000 a year there would be another rise. Land to the south of the station between the Aberdeen Railway sidings and the River Dee was then obtained by the Deeside Railway, and a goods station, sidings, and an engine shed laid out.

THE ALFORD DIVERSION

Having consolidated its position between Aberdeen and Banchory the directors now looked around for fresh fields to conquer—and their eyes fell on Alford. Situated to the north-west of Banchory, over the hills, Alford was—and is—a pleasant and prosperous market town by the River Don. As early as 1846 a line had been proposed to Alford from Kintore, to the east.

Unfortunately, the financial uncertainties of the mid-1840s affected this proposal, too, and before any construction could take place money became 'tight' and the Parliamentary powers which had been obtained lapsed, with nothing achieved. Later, in 1852, when the financial position had settled down again and the Great North main line was under construction between Kittybrewster and Huntly an attempt was made to revive the scheme, but there was little real progress. The promoters were wavering between three schemes when it became known that the Deeside Railway

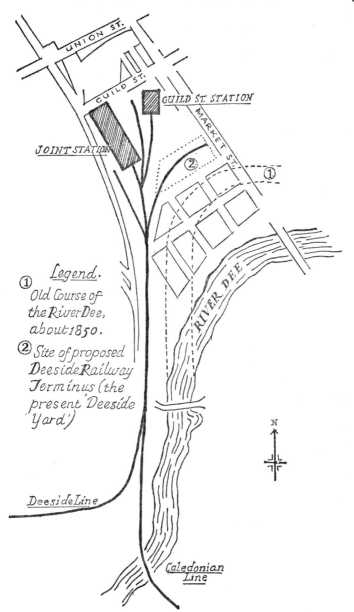

Map of the station area around Guild Street, Aberdeen

was contemplating an approach from the south. Immediately this was known, the original line from Kintore running through Tilly-fourie was selected for promotion.

Initially, the Deeside Company intended continuing its line from Banchory to Lumphanan and then *via* Cushnie to Alford—a total of sixteen miles. A survey was made of this route but it was then decided not to continue with it, but to promote a line from Coal-ford (or Culford), which was about three-quarters of a mile beyond Kennerty and some eight miles from Aberdeen. This hamlet was on the old Deeside Road and even in 1921 G. M. Fraser could say of it that it was 'scarcely known, even by name, nowadays'. The line was to pass through Echt and Tillyfourie, then follow the same route into Alford as the rival Alford Valley scheme. The proposed terminus was the same as for the Alford Valley Railway.

Proposals were also made to continue the line south again to Bridgetown. The distance from Coalford to Alford was twenty miles. A new company, the Deeside & Alford Valley Extension Railway, was promoted and was to be capitalised in 10,000 shares of £10 each. Notice of the intended Parliamentary Bill was published in the press and a meeting held in Alford to consider the rival schemes.

The Alford Valley proposal was now backed to the hilt by the Great North, which subscribed £15,000 and entered into a working agreement with the company. Despite these pressures the Deeside scheme was approved by an overwhelming majority of those who attended the meeting. Parliament—for neither the first nor the last time—decided to act against the majority opinion. Apart from the fact that the Alford Valley line would be shorter than that from Deeside it was decided by a select committee in Westminster that, notwithstanding the wishes of those concerned, the people of Alford would be better served by a railway leading into other parts of Aberdeenshire than by one to Deeside and thence to the county town. The Alford Valley Bill was therefore passed in June of 1856 and the fifteen-mile line eventually opened in March 1859.

THE FIRST EXTENSION

Despite the setback over the Alford Valley Extension, the Deeside Railway continued to prosper and, in 1856, opened another intermediate station at Ruthrieston, one and three-quarter miles from Guild Street. So prosperous was the company that it paid an increasing dividend through the years, and in 1857 this had reached 8½ per cent.

Although there were great happenings in the outside world at this time the business of promoting new railways went on apace, and the Deeside rebounded from its Alford defeat with another new Bill, less than a year later. This time the proposal was for an extension to Aboyne, where the original Act of 1846 had visualised the Deeside line terminating. On this occasion, the line was not planned to run through Kincardine O'Neil, but to strike in a more northerly direction, away from the river to Lumphanan, and then return south to enter Aboyne. As far as Lumphanan the route was very much the same as had first been planned for the start of the ill-fated Alford extension and no doubt the original survey made for that venture proved useful.

Although the new route enabled land to be purchased at considerably less expense than by the more direct way through Kincardine O'Neil, the line was two miles longer and involved some moderately heavy earthworks; also long stretches, particularly on each side of the summit by Lumphanan, were at a steep gradient.

In the *Aberdeen Journal* of 12 November 1856, there appeared a formal public notice of intention to lodge a Bill before Parliament in December. The Bill would seek powers to construct a railway

> commencing by a Junction with the rails of the main line of the said Deeside Railway, at a point thereon, at or near the West end of the Passenger Platform of the Banchory Station of the said Railway . . . and terminating in a Wood near the Mill of Aboyne.

It was proposed that the Deeside Railway should subscribe a sum of up to £5,000 from its existing funds towards the extension, and such further sums as were necessary would be raised by the issue of what was called postponed stock or by raising loans on the security of the Deeside Railway. Provision was also made for

> the blending and uniting, in one Capital Stock, the Capital Stocks of the said two undertakings if and when the same shall be deemed expedient, by the said Deeside Railway Company, and also to enable the said Deeside Railway Company to increase the number of their Directors to such extent as may be expedient, in the event of such union.

If deemed expedient it was proposed that a separate company could be incorporated 'for making and maintaining the Railway and works', and with powers to enter into 'Contracts and Agreements' with the Deeside Railway Company.

In due course the Bill was deposited and approved, and 'The

Deeside Railway Extension Act, 1857' received Royal Assent on 27 July of that year. The work was to be completed within three years.

The financial arrangements for the Deeside Extension Railway were, to say the least, unusual. It was in fact part of the Deeside Railway, was built by it and run by it at cost, but it had a different group of shareholders and the capital and stock of the two undertakings were to be kept separate, as were their accounts. These facts were used to run the two railways as virtually independent concerns.

Two new directors were elected to the board by, and to look after the interests of, the extension shareholders, but they could not vote on the dividends of the original shareholders who in turn could not vote on the extension dividends. Dividends on the two sections of the line were paid only on the profits of the section for which shares were held. As the extension was not such a financial success as the original line, this arrangement worked to the advantage of the original shareholders, who never received less than 5 per cent on their investment. The Act provided that, if and when the dividends of the two companies became equal, a three-fifths majority of the two groups of shareholders could vote for the amalgamation of the stock.

The first turf of the Extension Railway was cut on Friday, 2 October 1857 at Rosehill, about three-quarters of a mile below the village of Charleston of Aboyne. A large party of spectators having gathered, the proceedings commenced at two o'clock with prayer and, after a speech by John Duncan, the Marchioness of Huntly

> came forward, and, under the direction of Mr Willett, lifted the first sod in a graceful and 'workmanlike' manner, with an elegant spade prepared for the occasion, placing it on a very handsome barrow, bearing the Aboyne arms and motto, with the date 'October 2, 1857'. The sod was wheeled along the planks by Lord Aboyne (a fine-looking boy of eleven, in Highland costume) amid the hearty acclamations of the large assemblage of spectators.

After a few more words by the chairman, the company walked to the market square of Aboyne where, in a marquee, a luncheon was held at which the usual numerous toasts and speeches were given.

> The viands supplied by Mr Cook were excellent, as usual, and the champagne plentiful and good. The Banchory Band gave its services, and the presence of the fair sex rendered the success of the meeting complete.

Wine, women and song had again added zest to a basically mundane undertaking. The barrow and spade used by the Marchioness of Huntly have survived as have those of the 1852 ceremony, and are now preserved in Glasgow Transport Museum.

The Engineer of the new line was Mr Willett, with Mr Robertson as Resident Engineer, and Messrs Mitchell & Ireland as the contractor. The hope was expressed that the line would be open for traffic in about eighteen months, but this actually became two and a half years in the execution.

The total length of 15½ miles presented no very great engineering difficulties, although the gradients were severe. After leaving Banchory station a climb of 2½ miles, mostly at 1 in 68, began the ascent which continued at 1 in 70 to the summit at Tillychin (611 ft above sea level), where the line entered a cutting 50 ft deep and about a quarter of a mile long—known as Satan's Den. From there the run into Aboyne was mostly downhill, the gradient again being 1 in 70 or 71 for the first 2½ miles.

Apart from the cutting, the only other engineering work of note was the viaduct over the Beltie Burn, consisting of five arches each of 40 ft span. The station at Aboyne was actually built about half a mile beyond the authorised position to secure a more convenient site, and the line near Torphins had been built for over a mile outside the authorised limits. Parliament did not regularise these changes until The *Deeside* Railway Act of 30 June 1862 which also permitted an increase in capital of £24,000.

Finances for the Extension Railway were not so 'tight' as when the original line had been built and the station premises were of a more commodious and imposing style. At Aboyne itself (32¼ miles from Guild Street), the station was considered to be the last word in design. Intermediate stations were also supplied at Glassel (21⅜ miles from Guild Street), Torphins (23¾ miles) Lumphanan (26⅞ miles) and Dess (29½ miles), built in the same style as the rebuilt premises at Park and Crathes. The line was opened for public traffic the following Friday, 2 December, apparently without any further ceremony. The cost of construction had been £6,000 per mile, including land and station buildings, and 300,000 cu yd of earth had been excavated, including 97,000 cu yd from the Tillychin cutting alone. The contractor had been bound to have the works completed by March 1860, having begun work in March 1858 and thus finished three months ahead of schedule.

DEESIDE RAILWAY.

OPENING TO ABOYNE.

ALTERATION OF TRAINS.

ON and after FRIDAY, the 2d December, 1859, and until further notice, the Departures and Arrivals of PASSENGER TRAINS will be as follows, viz.:—

	1 Classes 1 & 3 Mail. A.M.	2 Classes 1 & 3 Mixed. A.M.	3 Classes 1 & 3 Mixed. P.M.	4 Classes 1 & 3 Mail. P.M.
Trains Depart				
From ABERDEEN (Guild Street Station)......	7·45	11·0	2·0	4·30
Arrive at BANCHORY...	8·50	12·15	3·30	5·32
Arrive at ABOYNE	9·45	1·22	...	6·42
Per Coach.				
Ballater............	11·45	...	...	...

** Seats per Coach to places beyond Aboyne may be secured at the Booking Office, Aberdeen.

Per Coach	Leaves				
	Ballater............	...	...	9·0	...
	Cambus O'May ...	...	...	9·35	...
	Dinnet	...	...	10·10	...

	1 Classes 1 & 3 Mixed. A.M.	2 Classes 1 & 3 Mail. A.M.	3 Classes 1 & 3 Mail. P.M.	4 Classes 1 & 3 P.M.
Trains Depart				
From ABOYNE	...	7·50	11·0	7·0
From BANCHORY	7·25	8·50	12·10	8·10
Arrive at ABERDEEN about............	9·0	9·50	1·30	9·15

For further information as to the Arrivals and Departures of Passenger Trains, Coaches running in connection, and Fares— see the Company's Time Table Books.

By order,
W. B. FERGUSON, Manager.

Deeside Railway Company's Offices,
Aberdeen, 29th November, 1859.

Announcement of the opening of the extension to Aboyne, 1859

INTERLUDE

Again a period of entrenchment intervened. In 1863 the privat platform for Crathes Castle and the small station at Mills of Drun were closed and to replace them a new public station was opene at Crathes on the site of the old platform.

One further projected railway may be mentioned here, althoug

Page 35: DRIVER'S-EYE VIEWS

(6) *'Satan's Den' cutting at Tillychin*
(7) *Approaching Lumphanan station*
(8) *The isolated station at Dess*
(9) *Approaching Dinnet*

Page 36: LINESIDE FEATURES

(10) *The old Ferry Inn at Cambus O'May, cut off to make way for the railway*
(11) *The end of the line at Ballater*

its story is more a part of railway politics than a potential improvement of the services to the area.

At this time relationships between the Scottish North Eastern Railway (which incorporated the Aberdeen Railway and its connection with the south) and the Great North of Scotland Railway in the north-east were distinctly poor. As a result of these two companies failing to agree on the provision of a joint station in Aberdeen, with through facilities to the north, the Scottish North Eastern Company projected a railway to link its main line at Limpet Mill, near Stonehaven, with Kintore thirteen miles to the north-west of Aberdeen and on the Great North's Alford Valley line.

This projected Scottish Northern Junction Railway—nominally independent, but in which the SNE was a joint promoter—was to cross the Deeside line west of Culter and connect with it by two spurs, one from the Stonehaven approach, leading to the western part of the Deeside line, and one from the Kintore approach, leading to the eastern section of the Deeside line, and to Aberdeen.

To obtain its through route to Kintore *via* Aberdeen, it was necessary that the SNJ should have the use of the Deeside line between Aberdeen and Culter, and negotiations were opened with a view either to lease the line or to obtain running powers over it. The story of the political intrigues surrounding these negotiations belongs in the next chapter. A Bill was introduced into Parliament for the session of 1862 seeking powers to construct the line, totalling eighteen miles (four miles less than the route to Kintore *via* Aberdeen).

Despite the opposition of the GNS and the Aberdeen Town Council, Royal Assent was given on 30 June 1862 to The *Scottish Northern Junction* Railway Act. A capital of £150,000 was authorised in £10 shares and the Scottish North Eastern Railway was permitted to subscribe up to £90,000 of this. The railway was to connect with the Deeside line from the north, commencing in a field near the farmhouse of Kennerty, to a point about 300 yd west of the viaduct over the Culter burn, and from the south at a point about 600 yd west from the west side of the bridge.

A period of five years was allowed for completing construction, and permission was given for the company to enter into agreements with the SNE to use and work the line. It was also required that the SNE, the GNS, and the Deeside Railway should make through bookings over the line. The sting lay in Section 40 of the Act. This provided that:

C

The Construction of the Railways shall be suspended until the First Day of *January* next, and if the *Great North of Scotland* Railway Company shall then have given the proper Notices, and deposited Plans and a Bill for constructing and completing within Three Years, at their own Expense, a Junction Railway between their Railway . . . and . . . the *Scottish North-eastern* Railway through or in the Vicinity of the City of *Aberdeen*, the Construction of the Railway shall be further suspended until such Bill is either passed, rejected, or withdrawn, and neither the *Scottish North-eastern* Railway Company, nor the Company shall directly or indirectly oppose such Bill . . . and in case such Bill shall be passed before the First Day of *September* One thousand eight-hundred and sixty-three, then the Railways hereby authorised shall not be constructed.

After considerable wrangling, an Act was eventually obtained in 1864 for the construction in Aberdeen of a joint station for through traffic, which was to act as a terminus for all three companies. The Scottish Northern Junction Railway was quietly allowed to pass into the collection of railways-that-never-were.

THE ABOYNE-BRAEMAR RAILWAY

It was inevitable that, when a railway as far as Aboyne proved successful, suggestions should be made for extending the line further up Deeside. Aboyne is only about half-way along the valley and, although the country beyond is more sparsely populated and less suitable for agriculture, there were nevertheless many attractions for the railway speculator. Apart from the valuable forests, and the village of Braemar itself, the Queen was now one of the landowners of the district and Her Majesty's presence at Balmoral was the foundation of a tourist industry that would grow with the years. Almost exactly four years after the opening of the extension to Aboyne, a notice appeared in the *Aberdeen Journal* of 16 November 1864, announcing the incorporation of a new company and giving details of a proposed Parliamentary Bill to build an 'Aboyne & Braemar Railway'.

The new company was entirely independent, although it was proposed to take powers

to enable the Company and the Deeside Railway Company to enter into and carry into effect such arrangements and agreements as they may think fit with reference to the construction, maintenance, and the working, management, running over, and use by the said Deeside Railway Company of the railway and works, for any term or terms of years, or in perpetuity.

Authority was also sought to enable the Deeside Company to 'subscribe to, and take, purchase, and hold shares in the Company or otherwise to contribute towards the expense of the Railway and works . . .' and to raise further capital for this purpose if necessary.

As originally envisaged in the notice, the new railway was to run from Aboyne 'at or near the west end of the Passenger Station at Aboyne, or Charleston of Aboyne, and terminating in the united Parish or Parishes of Crathie and Braemar, in the County of Aberdeen.'

After passing through a tunnel at the exit from Aboyne station, the line ran through 'the policies of Aboyne Castle' and crossed beneath the Tarland road. At Heughead about a mile further on the Deeside turnpike passed over the line which, after passing through the Muir of Dinnet, ran through Cambus O'May and thence, passing near Monaltrie House, to Ballater.

After leaving Ballater towards the farm of Balgairn, it would cross the Gairn Water and more or less follow the turnpike to a point just beyond the 55th milestone (half-way between the Danzig-Shiel bridge and General Wade's old bridge of Invercauld), where it would cross the river and follow the south bank for the remaining three miles into Braemar.

The station was to be about a quarter of a mile below the Invercauld Arms Hotel and on the same side of the road. The distance involved was about 28 miles and, although there cannot have been much hope of heavy traffic in the first instance, the proposed route was flat and involved no heavy engineering works once it had left Aboyne, so that construction and operating costs could be expected to be low. The Bill was duly deposited in December for consideration in the session of 1865.

The promoters' full intentions had been discussed widely and, as usual, two and two had been added together to make five. It was said that the eventual intention was to continue the line beyond Braemar and either pass through Glen Tilt to Blair Atholl, connecting with the Highland Railway, or—more ambitiously— through Glen Feshie to link with the Highland Railway at Kingussie, which was on the junction of a projected line to Fort William from the Inverness-Perth route, *via* Loch Laggan and Spean Bridge.

The difficulties of obtaining traffic for a Trans-Highland line, not to mention the extremely heavy engineering works that would have been involved, did not long keep people guessing, for early in the hearings before the select committee studying the Bill, counsel for the promoters specifically denied any intention of pressing westwards to link with the Highland Railway. Indeed, it was decided to take the line only as far as Bridge of Gairn, a distance of twelve and a half miles. The passenger terminus would be at Ballater and the remaining one and a half miles to the Gairn Water would be used for goods traffic only.

In this modified form 'An Act for making a Railway from the Deeside Railway Extension at *Charleston of Aboyne* to the *Bridge of Gairn*, to be called " *The Aboyne and Braemar* Railway" ' was given Royal Assent on 5 July 1865. It provided for a capital of £66,000 to be raised by 6,600 shares of £10 each and permitted the company to 'borrow on Mortgage any Sums not exceeding in the whole Twenty-two thousand Pounds'. The first directors were named as:

> James Ross Farquharson, William Brown and
> John Hickie (representing the shareholders)
> John Duncan, Sir Alexander Anderson and
> Peter Laing Gordon (representing the Deeside
> Railway Company).

The railway was to be completed within five years and the route was generally that which had been first proposed. Despite some suggestions that a route going first northwards from Aboyne through Coull to Tarland might prove more profitable, the line generally followed the new turnpike.

The total length of track authorised was 12 miles 4 furlongs, the section between Ballater and the Bridge of Gairn being authorised for goods traffic only. An important provision inserted was that

> No Extension of the Railway beyond the said Point distant Twelve Miles Four Furlongs from the said station at *Aboyne* shall be made up the Valley of the *Dee*, except under the Powers of a Local Act of Parliament to be specially obtained for that Purpose, and expressly authorising the same.

No such extension was in fact ever made. 'James Wright, Civil Engineer, Edinburgh, on behalf of the Promoters . . .' entered into an agreement with the Deeside Railway to build the line for a cost not exceeding £68,000 and then to hand it over to the Deeside, which would run it under control of a joint committee consisting of three directors of each company.

> The ceremony of cutting the first turf of the Aboyne and Braemar Railway took place on Thursday 7 September 1865 at Ballater, Mrs Farquharson of Invercauld wielding the silver spade on the

occasion, which was further made as enjoyable and attractive to the assemblage present as the glories of Highland scenery and the advantage of resplendent weather could make it.

After the usual prayer and speech the usual barrow, 'a handsome oak one, with the Invercauld crest and motto on the front', was produced and the usual 'official spade—silver with carved oak handle' used to lift the turf. By way of variety Mrs Farquharson herself 'wheeled off, and "tipped" over the bank . . . amid loud cheers of the assemblage'. Afterwards the usual dinner (at the Invercauld Arms Hotel, attended by 'about sixty gentlemen') was the occasion of the usual toasts and speeches, 'and the company broke up a little thereafter, the Aberdeen part of it coming on by special train from Aboyne at nine pm'.

The Engineer of the line was Mr J. W. Stewart, CE, and Mr Brownlees, CE, of London was Consulting Engineer. Kenneth Matheson of Dunfermline was the contractor, and he had agreed to finish the line by August 1866 for the sum of £50,000 as far as Ballater. The remaining one and a half miles to Bridge of Gairn 'will be completed simultaneously with the tramway, to be laid by Colonel Farquharson of Invercauld, who is Chairman of the new Company, for the accommodation of the Balmoral tenantry of the Queen, and his own tenantry'. More of this tramway later.

There were no great difficulties in the construction and the line was opened thirteen months later on 17 October 1866, 'much to the gratification of the Ballater folk, who turned out in considerable numbers on the occasion. There was no formal ceremony'. After leaving Aboyne station the line ran through a short tunnel of 127 yd length (the only one on the entire line) and thereafter the only engineering works of note were 'a considerable rock-cutting' at Cambus O'May and 'crossing the Tullich water by means of a malleable iron bridge of forty feet span'.

Although the engineering was not difficult the line was on a steadily-rising gradient. In the twelve miles of its route it rose 265 ft in height and Ballater station, at 660 ft above sea level, became the new summit of the line from Aberdeen. An intermediate station was provided at Dinnet (36¾ miles from Guild Street) half a mile west of the site originally proposed and in what has been described as 'splendid isolation'. The station at Ballater (43¼ miles from Aberdeen) was small, consisting only of a booking office and one platform, which would scarcely accommodate the Royal train, although in 1899 a signalbox was added.

In September 1866, as a result of political wrangling that will be recorded elsewhere, the Deeside Railway was leased to the GNS, which ran the services over the Aboyne & Braemar Railway as the Deeside's lessee.

Beyond Ballater the works had never been very far advanced, and after the line was opened work on the extension to Bridge of Gairn was suspended. About eighteen months later James Ross Farquharson of Invercauld made an agreement with the three railways concerned—the Aboyne & Braemar, the Deeside, and the Great North of Scotland—by which he undertook to complete the line to the Gairn Water and connect it with the tramway that he intended building from there to a point about twelve miles towards Braemar, for carrying timber from Ballochbuie forest. The line was completed for about one and a quarter miles, beginning in a cutting beyond Ballater station. Other works included masonry retaining walls beside the river and a bridge over the Gairn Water. Although the track was laid it was never used, nor was the connecting tramway built.

THE BALLATER-BRAEMAR MYSTERY

Why the line was not completed beyond Ballater has long been debated, it frequently being alleged that the reason was Queen Victoria's objection to the presence of a railway along the edge of her Balmoral estate.

On 7 April a public meeting was held in the Mason's Hall, Ballater, 'of the inhabitants of the Ballater and Braemar district, in favour of an extension of the Deeside Railway to Ballater'. There was a large attendance and the Chairman, Mr Brown, the factor of the Invercauld Estates, told it:

> You are all aware that the object of this meeting is to draw up resolutions in favour of the proposed extension of Railway from Aboyne to here . . . you are aware that the Bill, as first brought before the House of Commons, was called 'The Aboyne and Braemar Railway'; but this has been somewhat altered. Owing to circumstances not easily explainable, opposition of an unreasonable and peculiar nature, little expected, and also in my opinion for want, perhaps, of thorough enthusiasm by its promoters, the original paper will, I believe, be clipt down to 'The Aboyne and Ballater Railway Extension'. These are about the plain facts of the story.

This is the first indication we have that the line as far as Braemar was not to be pressed, and there seems little doubt that Mr Brown's devious wording referred to opposition from the Royal landowner at Balmoral. After several speeches listing the advantages of the proposed line two resolutions were passed in support of the scheme.

> The Chairman then suggested that a respectful memorial should be transmitted to Her Majesty, embodying the sense of what had passed at the meeting, and asking her to accord her gracious approval of the proposed railway (Applause). Such a course would let Her Majesty know the feeling in the district (Applause).

Those present obviously knew where the opposition lay.

On Thursday, 11 May 1865 at Westminster, the committee for Group 21 of private bills met and considered the Bill. There were three petitions against the proposed railway. These had been entered by a

> Mrs Shepherd of Craigendarroch, who occupies a house on the line of railway, but who had not put in any appearance in support of her petition . . . the Trustees of the Aboyne and Ballater Road, which is founded mainly upon objections in regard to engineering matters, which have already been disposed of by the referees. Then there was the petition of the Marchioness of Huntly.

Mr Bircham, as agent for the Marchioness, promised the committee:

> I think we shall not require to give any further trouble. An arrangement has been made, but not signed; and if I have an understanding in this room that the agreement is settled, we shall make no further appearance.

The nature of the agreement soon became clear. For the promoters, Mr Milward, QC, said: 'The line, as proposed, would pass, as was well known, near Balmoral. There was an objection, however, to its being carried so far as a locomotive line, and he was now prepared to renew an offer made previously to stop the locomotive and passenger department of the line at a point which would relieve almost all the objections made to carrying the line farther, namely at Ballater.

For goods and minerals, which were of great importance to the railway, it was proposed that a tramway should be continued to Bridge of Gairn, a little farther up.' And so it was arranged. Beyond Ballater there would be only a tramway as far as Bridge of Gairn, and the company agreed that, 'if we wish to extend beyond Bridge of Gairn, we bind ourselves that we shall come to Parliament for a special Act'.

That the local people were in no doubt as to who was really

responsible for the truncation of the scheme is shown in the report of the cutting of the first turf, which appeared in the *Aberdeen Journal* of 13 September 1865, where the unknown reporter referred to the company which, 'in deference to the wishes of Royalty, consented, when their Bill was in Committee of the Commons last spring, to limit it at present to Bridge of Gairn'. Even the need for extending a tramway as far as Bridge of Gairn for the timber traffic was eliminated in 1866 or thereabouts, for the Ballochbuie forests were bought by the Queen and there was then no need for exploitation of their timber.

The old suspicions that Queen Victoria was personally responsible for the termination of the railway at the Gairn Water have now been confirmed. The author has recently discovered, in the minute books of the Deeside Railway Company, details of 'an arrangement between the Promoters of the Aboyne & Braemar Railway and Mr Arnold William White on behalf of Her Majesty the Queen'. This 'arrangement' is minuted following the directors' meeting on 28 May 1865 and provides that it shall

> Not be lawful for the Company to take, or use, either compulsorily or by agreement any of the said lands or property situate to the Westward of a point distant twelve miles four furlongs from the existing passenger station at Aboyne.

It further goes on to provide that

> The Promoters and when incorporated the Aboyne and Ballater Railway Company to come under obligations not at any time hereafter to apply for or promote or in any way directly or indirectly assist in the formation or working of any Railway up the Valley of the Dee for Passenger traffic above the said proposed terminal station at Ballater or for Goods traffic above the proposed terminus on the Westside of the Bridge of Gairn.

The price paid for this limitation was that

> In consideration of the above stipulations Mr Arnold William White to procure withdrawal of the opposition . . . against the Bill as amended.

The agreement was signed by John Duncan and Arnold William White, who is described as 'Private Solicitor to Her Majesty the Queen'.

It is quite clear from the above quotations that the Queen herself (through the medium of her private solicitor) had arranged to protect her privacy at Balmoral, as was suspected at the time.

Page 45 : STATION ARCHITECTURE

(12) *Park station*
(13) *Rural beauty at Cambus O'May*
(14) *Victorian splendour at Aboyne*

Page 46 : BALLATER STATION

(15) *No 14 in the bay, around* 1910
(16) *D40 No 62275, just after nationalisation*
(17) *Diesel multiple-unit in the station,* 1965

Page 47 : BANCHORY STATION
(18) *The original station*, 1901
(19) *During rebuilding*, 1902
(20) *The station as rebuilt*

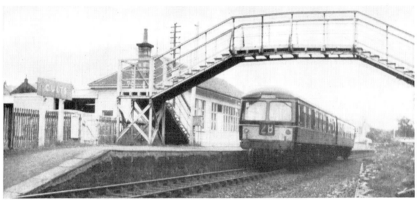

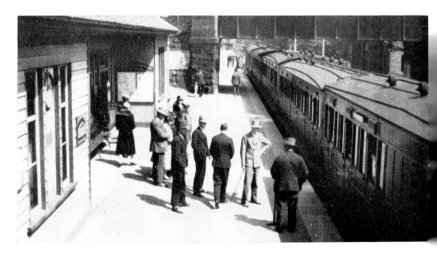

Page 48: CULTS AND CULTER

(21) *Cults station, 1920*
(22) *Cults just before closure* (1965)
(23) *Culter. The first Sunday suburban train* (1928)

ENTRENCHMENT

In 1864 a long period of disagreement between the Great North and the Scottish North Eastern Railways over a junction and station facilities terminated when an Act was obtained permitting the construction of a joint station. This was situated near the Guild Street station of the SNE, and connected to the GNS station at Kittybrewster by a line through the Denburn. As lessee of the Deeside Railway, the GNS had by 1866 the use of Guild Street and was now enabled to bring all its services into one terminal.

With the works by the Gairn Water, the construction of railways in the Dee valley virtually finished, and from this point on the energies of the various companies which successively controlled the line were directed solely to improvements.

In 1876 a second intermediate station was opened on the Aboyne—Ballater line at Cambus O'May ($39\frac{3}{4}$ miles from Aberdeen). It was a simple platform at first beside a ballast pit, and was used as a halt; a small building was added later. Cambus O'May was one of the most picturesque railway stations in the country, with the river running beneath it and the wooded hills all around.

It was also in 1876 that the Great North of Scotland Railway finally amalgamated the Deeside and Aboyne & Braemar Railways, as will be told in the next chapter, and it was that company which was responsible for nearly all the subsequent improvements. Increased traffic and the gradual opening up of lower Deeside as a residential area necessitated doubling of the original single line and powers to do this over the first ten miles from Ferryhill to Park were obtained in 1877, but because of financial stringencies this work was not put in hand and an extension of time for completion of the work had to be obtained.

Eventually the first two and three-quarter miles, as far as West Cults, were completed on 14 June 1884. Land for the rest of the widening was obtained but expenditure throughout the GNS system on track widening had been very heavy in the early 1880s—so much so that between 1881 and 1883 no dividends were paid on ordinary shares and for the next ten years the dividends were extremely low. In 1892, the doubling was extended to Murtle on 13 July and, ten weeks later, to Culter on 24 September.

One further scheme for a railway to link with the Deeside line remains to be described. Unlike the stillborn Deeside & Alford Valley Extension Railway already described, the new venture was by a company unrelated to that on Deeside or Strathspey—its two terminal areas.

The GNS system lay across the north-east of Scotland like a huge horseshoe, with the two ends of the open part at Ballater and Boat of Garten. Although only thirty miles apart as the crow flies, there were 144½ miles of railway between them around the 'U', and the proposed Strathspey, Strathdon & Deeside Junction Railway was intended to join this gap by linking the two lines in Strathspey and Deeside between their penultimate stations at Nethy Bridge and Cambus O'May, and would thus have made the Great North route into a complete circle.

The proposed railway was promoted by a group of landowners from Deeside and Donside led by the Marquis of Huntly, through whose lands the Aboyne & Braemar Railway already ran. The prospectus, published in the *Aberdeen Free Press* of 16 November 1883, proposed

> A Railway commencing in the Parish of Abernethy and Kincardine, in the County of Inverness, by a junction with the Strathspey Section of the Great North of Scotland Railway, near the Northern end of the Nethy Bridge Station . . . and terminating . . . by a junction with the Deeside Section of the Great North of Scotland Railway, west of Dinnet Station.

Powers were sought to enable the GNS to work the line and to require them to make through bookings over it. The proposed route required some very heavy engineering works—for example, four tunnels, one of them 3,190 yd long between the Avon and the Don, and a summit level of 1,500 ft above sea level, which was greater than that of any other British railway. The heaviest gradient would have been 1 in 56.

The estimated cost of £600,000 would probably have been exceeded in constructing this line which in truth had little potential as a revenue earner, as it passed through mainly barren and uninhabited country. Some idea of the nature of this country may be had from comparing the 30 mile straight-line distance of its terminal points with the forty-two miles of track necessary to cross it. Scenically this line would have outdone even the famous West Highland line, but financially it would have been disastrous. Parliament saw this and rejected the scheme, which joined the list of unbuilt railways which even a small line like the Deeside was gathering around it.

By now, the growing residential districts around Aberdeen were reaching the point at which regular suburban train services were called for and such a service was begun on the Deeside line in 1894. For this service stations were opened at Holburn Street ($1\frac{3}{8}$ miles from the joint station), Pitfodels (3 miles) and West Cults ($4\frac{1}{8}$ miles). In 1897, the spread of the suburban population and increasing prosperity of the area was reflected in the opening of another station at Bieldside ($4\frac{3}{4}$ miles) adjacent to the golf course.

After some years, the rather primitive conditions at Ballater station drew a letter (dated 14 October 1884) from Mr J. T. McKenzie of Glenmuick to the chairman. In this, Mr McKenzie suggested that the provision of a special Royal waiting room for Her Majesty would be a much-appreciated kindness. He wrote:

> The expense could only be a trifle for making a small room of the kind required, and would appear, as a Kindly offer of respect coming unsolicited from the Railway. Should the Railway not have the funds to do so, I have no doubt other Railways drawing advantage from the traffic would gladly contribute although I think you will agree with me it would look better coming from the Deeside Railway alone if you could manage it, and for this reason I make the letter private to you, that if done it should appear to be the spontaneous action of the Railway.

This dig obviously stung the Great North into action, for within a month the directors were perusing plans of the Royal waiting room at Sandringham and by December plans for a similar room at Ballater were shown to the Queen, who indicated her approval of them. Ballater station was rebuilt in 1886 and became the only one in Scotland to boast an example of this little-used but impressive facility. So pleased was Mr McKenzie with the railway's action that he offered to supply it with the stone for rebuilding the station free of charge, although in the event it was rebuilt with timber. A roof was added over part of the platform and a porch at the entrance from the station yard. A refreshment room was later added and thereafter the station remained virtually unaltered until it was closed in 1966.

In 1897, powers were obtained in the Great North of Scotland Railway Act of 15 July

> for the Company to erect and establish and to manage or to let on lease for any term not exceeding twenty-one years a hotel in connection with their station at Ballater and to apply for that purpose any of their existing funds.

Unfortunately, this scheme never came into fruition. Later in the year a suggestion that an hotel be built at Glengairn met with the Queen's disapproval, and although 'plans for a new hotel and station buildings at Ballater' were considered nothing ever came of the scheme (GNS Finance Committee minutes, 2 March and 8 June 1898).

The doubling of the line continued and, on 28 August 1899, this reached Park. No further double-line sections were ever opened on Deeside, although powers were obtained in the Great

Seal of the Aboyne & Braemar Railway Company

North of Scotland Railway Act of 1898 to widen the track from Park to Banchory at an estimated cost of £38,100. Plans for the work were deposited, but it was never put in hand. Also in 1899, the iron girder bridge over the Leuchar burn at Culter was replaced with a short single-span steel girder bridge running between embankments.

Almost the last act of major improvement on the Deeside line was the rebuilding of Banchory station during 1902 to more or less its present appearance but about 100 yd west of the original site. At the same time a new engine shed and carriage sheds were provided. Virtually nothing more was added to the line for over half a century until British Railways provided a new halt, also at Banchory. The original station had always been inconveniently far from the town centre and the new platform, a timber erection only 29 ft long and with a single old GNS oil lamp as its only adornment, was situated at Dee Street, 17½ miles from the joint station and intended to remedy the falling passenger receipts. It was not even long enough to take the two-car diesel multiple-units then in use on the line. Opened in February 1961, it was closed when the whole line was finally closed to passenger traffic, exactly five years later, in February 1966.

CHAPTER 3

A Hundred and Thirteen Years

CHANGES OF OWNERSHIP

The formation of the companies which built the line from Aberdeen to Ballater has already been described and, until 1866, the Deeside Railway Company ran both its own line as far as Banchory and that of the extension railway to Aboyne.

Despite the separate financial arrangements for the extension, the concern was run as one railway. The original Deeside line was always a prosperous affair, and the shrewdness of the directors in insisting on separate finances for the extension was shown by the much lower dividend which it returned. The original stock returned five per cent for the first five years of operation, and this gradually rose to seven and one quarter per cent in 1862, and remained at seven per cent until 1865. The extension stock returned two per cent in its first year, nothing at all for the next two years, and only two per cent thereafter.

Two years after the extension to Aboyne was opened, the Deeside Railway was able to take advantage of a bitter disagreement between the other two companies in the area. The Aberdeen Railway, which had helped the Deeside Company so much in its early days, had in July 1856 amalgamated with the Scottish Midland Junction Railway to form the Scottish North Eastern Railway Company, and this was at loggerheads with the Great North of Scotland Railway over the provision of a junction between the two systems.

It was in this heated atmosphere that the Scottish North Eastern launched the plans for the Scottish Northern Junction Railway already described. By reaching to Kintore directly and avoiding Aberdeen it thus hoped to solve the *impasse*. More importantly, if it could obtain the desired connections with the Deeside line just west of Culter, it would then have a direct route north from its own terminus at Guild Street, *via* the Deeside, and so completely bypass the Great North system.

For this scheme to work it was necessary that the Scottish North Eastern should either lease, or at the least acquire running powers over, the Deeside Railway, and to this end negotiations were opened with the Deeside company. In view of the previous happy relations between the two companies one would have expected negotiations to be brief, friendly and favourable. In fact, the outcome was a surprising change of loyalties by the Deeside which was to isolate it administratively from the railway to the south for 81 years.

The extreme bitterness which the dispute over the control of the Deeside line engendered has been lost sight of with the passage of time, but at the time of the negotiations the term 'railway warfare' that was used to describe the situation was, if anything, an understatement.

After introducing its Scottish Northern Junction Railway Bill in November 1861, the Scottish North Eastern approached the Deeside Company for running powers over that line. It was agreed by the Deeside Board that these should be granted, subject to reasonable rates being agreed and, 'to avoid any imputations of favouritism from the Great North of Scotland Railway Company, they were prepared to give that Company similar powers, if desired'.

Negotiations for fixing the rate took place and, although the usual rate in such cases was said to be about 65 per cent of the gross traffic carried, the Deeside Company asked only 47 per cent. The Scottish North Eastern offered 30 per cent at first, and although subsequently raising this to 35 per cent, refused to go beyond that. It appears that at this point John Duncan personally approached the Great North of Scotland Railway and, as a result, this latter company offered to lease the Deeside Railway. On learning this the SNE raised its offer to 47 per cent for running powers, but by then John Duncan had accepted the GNS offer.

It was now claimed that the running powers sought by the SNE 'were calculated to disturb and embarrass the local traffic on the Deeside line', and it was suggested to that company that only a lease could meet the occasion. The terms suggested were eight per cent dividend for the Deeside and four per cent for the Extension. The SNE declined these terms as excessive, and refused to lease the Extension 'on *any terms, as worthless and undesirable*'.

As no counter terms were offered, the Deeside directors—or at any rate, some of them—'had no hesitation thereafter in receiving

Deeside Railway.

PRIVATE

TIME TABLE

OF THE

PASSENGER AND GOODS TRAINS

FOR THE

Guidance of the Company's Servants only,

TO BE OBSERVED

On and after 1st JUNE, 1858,

Till further notice.

☞ *Time-Bills of an earlier date to be destroyed.*

Every Officer and Servant must make himself conver-
sant with this Table, in order that he may be thoroughly
acquainted with all Alterations that may have been made.

No Irregular Train, or Ordinary Goods Train, if out of
proper time, shall be despatched from Aberdeen, until the
Superintendent, or other person in charge at the Goods Station, has first communicated with the Superintendent of the
Passenger Station.

NOTE.—The hours stated in the Tables are those at which
the Trains ought to *start* from the various Stations. Engine-
men must therefore endeavour to *arrive* in time to allow of
the times of departure being punctually adhered to.

GENERAL MANAGER'S OFFICE
ABERDEEN.

ABERDEEN TO BANCHORY.

Miles.	Trains will not depart from, nor arrive at. the following Stations before the Hours undernoted respectively.	DOWN TRAINS.				
		1. 1 & 3 Class Mail.	2. 1 and 3 Class.	3. Mixed 1 & 3 Class	4. 1 & 3 Class Mail.	5. 1 & 3 Class.
	TRAINS LEAVE	A.M.	A.M.	P.M	P.M.	P.M.
	Aberdeen,	7.45	11.0	1.45	4.15*	7.0
	Ruthrieston,	7.52	—	—	—	7.7
	Cults,	8.0	11.15	2.5	4.29	7.15
	Murtle,	8.4	11.20	2.12	4.34	7.19
	Milltimber,	—	11.25	2.19		7.23
	Culter,	8.11	11.29	2.29	4.40	7.27
	Drum,		11.41	2.45	4.52	7.37
	Park,	8.22	11.46	2.50	4.57	7.41
	Mills of Drum,	8.30	11.54	2.55	5.5	7.50
	Banchory, arrive at	8.40	12.5	3.15	5.15	8.0

Coach Arrives at Potarch about	10.0	...	...	6.30	...
Do. Kincardine O'Neil,	10.15	...	...	6.50	..
Do. Aboyne,	10.46	...	...	7.30	...
Do. Ballater,	12.28 P.M.	..	...	...	...

Coach Leaves Ballater,	...	...	8.30	...	...
Do. Aboyne,	...	6.45	10.0	...	...
Do. Banchory, arrive	...	8.45	12.10	...	...

BANCHORY TO ABERDEEN.

Miles.	Trains will not depart from, nor arrive at. the following Stations before the Hours undernoted respectively.	UP TRAINS				
		1. Mixed 1 & 3 Class.	2. 1 & 3 Class Mail.	3. 1 and 3 Class. Mail.	4. 1 & 3 Class.	5 1 & 3 Class.
	TRAINS LEAVE	A.M.	A.M.	P.M.	P.M.	P.M.
	Banchory,	7.20	8.57	12.30	5.45	8.30
	Mills of Drum,	7.32	9.6	12.40	—	8.40
	Park,	7.43	9.13	12.48	6.0	8.48
	Drum,	7.49	9.17	12.53		8.52
	Culter,	8.0	9.24	1.3	6.10	9.3
	Milltimber,	8.18	—	1.8	—	9.8
	Murtle,	8.25	9.30	1.12	6.16	9.13
	Cults,	8.32	9.37	1.18	6.23	9.20
	Ruthrieston,				—	9.27
	Aberdeen, arrive at	8.55	9.50	1.30	6.35	9.35

* ☞ ON SATURDAYS, No. 4 Down Train will leave Aberdeen at 4.30 p.m. instead of 4.15 p.m., arriving at all the other Stations 15 minutes later than usual.

Nos. 1. and 3. Up Trains will stop only by Signal at Drum and Milltimber when there are Goods or Passengers to forward or put off

No. 1. Up Train will shunt at Culter to allow No. 1. Down Train to pass.

working timetable, 1858

D

overtures from the Great North, which ended in the agreement for lease'. The GNS offered 'six per cent of guaranteed Dividend for the Deeside line, with such additional dividend as may be payable on the ordinary stock of the Great North to its own shareholders'. By the agreement the Great North of Scotland undertook to work the Extension line 'as at present' (Directors' report to the general meeting, 1862).

Not unnaturally, the Scottish North Eastern took a poor view of these arrangements and immediately offered to purchase 'such an amount of the Extension Shares as would have obstructed . . . the lease to the Great North'. This failing, it then made an improved offer for a lease as follows:

FOR THE DEESIDE	FOR THE EXTENSION
7 per cent for 2 years	2 per cent for 2 years
7½ per cent for 3rd year	2½ per cent for each year following till 6th
8 per cent thereafter	4 per cent thereafter

and then 'on that being rejected, of another on still higher terms'. This offer increased the former one for the Extension, to:

3 per cent for the first 2 years
3½ per cent for the 3rd year
4 per cent for the 4th year
4½ per cent thereafter.

The difference between this offer and the estimated return from the Extension traffic for the first two years (2½ per cent), was thus about ½ per cent in favour of the Scottish North Eastern offer, but the limitation of the dividend to 4½ per cent on and after the fifth year was an objection. In fact the Great North had purchased £30,000 worth of unallocated Extension stock, together with £12,000 worth which John Duncan had quietly sold to them— the whole of his personal holding in the Extension. As the Chairman also held by his own admission, 'as much as 50 per cent of all the stock held by all the tenants on Deeside', he and the Great North together could out-vote any opposition.

The board of the Deeside Railway was deeply divided over the issue, and in a summary of these negotiations submitted as a report to an extraordinary general meeting of the company held on 13 May 1862, and already quoted above, it said:

The differences of opinion at the Board are to be regretted; but one thing is certain, the supporters of the Lease to the Great North of Scotland Company hold by far the larger stake in the Deeside and Deeside Extension . . . in conclusion, the terms of the working agreement and lease now submitted for your approval, have been sanctioned by the shareholders of the Great North . . . they are approved by a preponderating majority of both stocks of the Deeside Company.

While it is true that John Duncan and the GNS, in terms of shares held, could out-vote the entire general meeting, the Deeside board was equally divided, and there were 319 shareholders, of which 240 had sent proxies to the meeting to vote against the lease to the Great North. Further, the Great North shareholders had not in fact accepted the terms of the lease as the Deeside report had stated; this was not done until an extraordinary general meeting of the Great North a fortnight later on 27 May. The stage was set for a right royal row and, at the general meeting of the Deeside Company on 13 May, the storm broke.

John Duncan was in no doubt about his own unpopularity over the move. Right at the beginning of the meeting he described himself as 'the best abused man in the North of Scotland'. He went on to argue his case for leasing to the Great North, and impugned the motives of his opponents.

Even Duncan's staunch friend and ally, Patrick Davidson, the Deputy-Chairman, when called on to second the motion for acceptance, declined to include in his seconding, acceptance of the report, which had certainly been written in the most partisan of terms. He went on: 'It is clear that Mr Duncan and the Great North have the matter in their own hands, and that they can carry, or oppose the carrying, of anything'. Immediately the motion was seconded Mr Smith of Glenmillan rose to move an amendment, that the agreement 'be not approved of'.

From here on, personal 'slanging' became the theme of the meeting. It was revealed that the board had been equally divided and that the chairman's casting vote had been used to reject the Scottish North Eastern proposals. Mr Smith informed the meeting that he had informed the board—as an extension director—that he 'would hold those voting against the better (ie, SNE) offer as personally liable to them in the consequences'. He went on: 'I find, from higher level authority than my own, that we have a remedy at law (Applause). I hope matters will not come to such a pass; but I allude to this to let you know what passed at the Board'.

It was said that the Deeside 'should have more honour about us than desert the Scottish North Eastern Company', and the ability of the Great North to pay its obligations was questioned. It was also revealed that John Duncan and three of the Deeside directors had been put on the provisional committee for the Scottish Northern Junction Railway, although their report stated that 'there was nothing in this scheme favourable to Deeside Railway interests'. In short, the chairman was being accused of playing off one side against the other for his own ends.

The directors' report, said one speaker, 'contained language such as one gentleman would not use to another; and besides, he ventured to say, it was not the language of truth'. The meeting was gradually becoming more acrimonious.

Accusation followed accusation, shareholders calling one another liars and 'not gentlemen', and the board was accused of discourtesy to the shareholders. The final vote was delayed, 'the meeting having almost entirely broken up . . . (it now being twenty minutes past four)' owing to 'numbers leaving to catch the Deeside train', but John Duncan got his approval. Although the number of votes cast were 3,255 against 1,341, this represented shares held and 187 persons actually had their way over 276; and, of the 187, the Great North had nominated 106 by virtue of their newly-bought stock.

Commenting on the *fracas* in an editorial column the following week, the *Aberdeen Journal* stated:

> We cannot say that the fight, such as it was, gives us a high idea of the principles of inter-railway policy, which seems even more exclusively self-seeking than the practical interpretation of International Law. The Scottish North-Eastern appears to have lost the Deeside by making too low an offer, and the Great North of Scotland to have got it by slipping in a secret offer, with a *solatium* for the individual services and sacrifices of the gentlemen on whom the decision mainly depended.

It referred to 'the flattest contradictions, the sharpest recriminations' which had been bandied around the Deeside meeting, and concluded that, finally to settle the 'railway warfare' an Aberdeen Junction between the two main protagonists was 'the only measure which can prevent the Great North and the North Eastern devoting their energies to the work of cutting each other's throats . . . Without it there will be war for ten years to come . . .'

One battle may have been lost but, so far, the war was not won, for the Scottish North Eastern decided that, before the matter came before Parliament for ratification, it would take steps to prevent implementation of the lease and, on application to the Lord Ordinary of the Court of Session, an interdict was granted prohibiting the parties from carrying the agreement into operation on the ground of its illegality. A further interdict was also obtained by the three dissenting members of the Deeside Board on the grounds that the company had no authority by its original Acts to delegate its powers. The cost of this interdict was paid by the SNE. This meant that for the present the lease could not be put into effect, and that the matter had to be thrashed out before Parliament.

At the Deeside's annual general meeting on the following 23 October, John Duncan waxed indignant at the actions of the Scottish North Eastern and of the minority of his own board, and again a great deal of personal rancour was expressed, but John Duncan had the last word and a set of more compliant directors was elected.

Bringing the proposed lease before Parliament was a lengthy process, and it was not until the session of 1866 that the matter reached Westminster. In the meantime, John Duncan was duly rewarded by the Great North for services rendered. In 1864 he was elected to its board of directors and appointed deputy chairman.

In the period 1865-6, many amalgamations of small railways with their larger neighbours took place and the Scottish North Eastern was very involved in its proposed amalgamation with the Caledonian Railway. The story of this particular struggle has already been told elsewhere, but the SNE entry into the Caledonian rather than the North British fold was to affect the Deeside line profoundly for many years to come.

At this same time the Great North of Scotland was engaged in its own round of amalgamations of all minor railways in its territory, and into the Bill it slipped a provision for lease of the Deeside Railway. At the annual general meeting of the Great North on 5 April 1866, the Chairman, Sir J. D. H. Elphinstone, expressed surprise that the Scottish North Eastern was to oppose its Bill, although he also announced that with regard to the SNE Bill for amalgamation with the Caledonian—'in the interests of your Company, gentlemen, we intend to oppose'. It is no wonder that the GNS was not the most popular or best understood of railway companies. As the *bel ami* of the Great North, the Deeside Railway also opposed the Caledonian merger.

When the committee on Group 20 of Private & Local Bills met on 11 June, the main lines of argument were that the Scottish North Eastern was engaged in becoming part of a great through route, while the Great North—having been cheated of its through connection to Inverness—was now concerned mainly with local traffic and, as the Deeside was essentially a local line, it more naturally belonged to the GNS sphere of influence.

There was disagreement when the Scottish North Eastern alleged that the Deeside carried more than 10,000 tons a year of traffic from it, against 800 tons from the Great North, and a reference was made to the refusal of the Great North to make good connections with the SNE trains. The chairman of the committee shrewdly observed that 'it is very clear the companies are not friendly together.'

The position was put clearly by Mr Denison for the SNE: 'Here is a company coming up with a thing declared by the courts to be illegal, and upon which they have slept for four years, yet they ask to be put in a position to carry it out'. Yet the committee decided in favour of the Bill, subject to some adjustment of the clauses regarding the joint station, and it was passed on into the legislative machine. The whole three days of the hearings had been taken up with the Deeside lease, there being no objections to the other amalgamations proposed.

The terms of the lease were attached to The Great North of Scotland Railway (Amalgamation) Act, 1866, which received Royal Assent on 30 July 1866. Under section 45 it was enacted that

> The Deeside Railway Company may grant to the Company and the Company may accept a Lease of the Undertaking . . . upon the Terms and Conditions contained in the Agreement for Lease of which a Copy is set forth in the Schedule (C) to this Act, and which Agreement is hereby confirmed and made binding upon the Two Companies.

The Act also confirmed the right of the Great North, as lessee, to enjoy the running powers of the Deeside over the Scottish North Eastern track between Ferryhill and Guild Street, and joint use of the SNE terminus. The agreement referred to (Schedule C to the Act) provided that 'The Lease shall be for a Term of Nine hundred and ninety-nine Years, and shall commence and take Effect from the First Day of September next'.

The financial terms arranged were not unreasonable. A dividend of $7\frac{1}{2}$ per cent was guaranteed on the original stock, and on the Extension stock a dividend of 3 per cent for the first year and $3\frac{1}{2}$ per cent thereafter. It was further agreed that, if in any year the gross revenues of the Deeside and its Extension should exceed £27,000, one half of that excess should go to the Great North and the other half to the Deeside, where it would be distributed in the ratio of 17/32 to the original shareholders and 15/32 to the Extension shareholders.

On its part the Great North was also required to

> use the best Endeavours to accommodate, develop, extend, and increase the Traffic of the said Undertakings, and maintain and keep for the Service of the Deeside Railway Company at least an equal Quantity and Value of Rolling Stock, and in order to the better Identification of the said Rolling Stock the same shall continue to be marked and lettered with the Name of the Deeside Railway Company, and shall at all Times be maintained as a separate and distinct Plant.

To arrange all these matters a joint committee was set up, consisting of three members chosen by each of the two boards. This committee also had the task of arranging train workings, which were to be no less than had operated before, and neither were the fares to be increased 'without the express Approval of a Majority of the Members of the said Joint committee appointed by the Board of the Deeside Railway Company'.

The lease applied only to the line as far as Aboyne, the Aboyne & Braemar Railway being an independent company. As the lease became operative some seven weeks before the opening of this latter railway its agreement for the Deeside Railway to run it was actually implemented by the Great North, as lessee.

In 1868, John Duncan received the fulness of his reward and was elected Chairman of the Great North of Scotland Railway Company, while at the same time remaining Chairman of the Deeside Company and Deputy-Chairman of the Aboyne & Braemar. His very busy life was beginning to catch up with Duncan by now and, in 1872, after only four years in the Great North chair he was obliged by ill-health to vacate the office, although he retained his seat on the board and his chairmanship of the Deeside company. He did not long survive after leaving the Great North chairmanship, for he died of a bronchial condition on 12 December 1874, just over two years later, aged seventy-three years and three months.

It was ironic that, after working so hard towards making the Deeside line an integral part of the Great North system, Duncan should not live to see the final stage of amalgamation of the companies. After the junction between (and construction of a joint station for the use of) the Great North and the Caledonian was opened in 1867 the traffic on the Deeside line not surprisingly increased, and the resultant need for track re-laying and other improvements led to a number of financial problems regarding the proportions of cost to be paid by the owning and leasing companies. The independent status of the somewhat impoverished Aboyne & Braemar Railway was also giving rise to some problems, particularly as the agreement for the Deeside Railway to work the line expired in October of 1876.

The matter was brought to the attention of the general meeting of the Deeside Railway on 21 October 1876 when Patrick Davidson of Inchmarlo, who had succeeded John Duncan as Chairman, read a letter which he had received from the Chairman of the Great North. It was dated 8 October and is worth quoting in full:

Dear Sir, In consequence of the great increase which has taken place in the traffic of the Deeside Railway, it is necessary for the safety and accommodation of the public that a considerable expenditure should be incurred in enlarging the stations and sidings. Some of the trains in summer are now so large that neither the platforms nor sidings are at all adequate for them, and there is often serious risks of accidents arising from such a state of matters. There is no provision in the agreement for the lease of the line to this Company for the raising and expending of any additional capital required for such purposes. In fact, it seems not to have been in the view of the parties at the time the agreement was negotiated that the traffic would increase to such an extent as to require the expenditure of additional capital, and neither Company have such capital or the power to raise it. The land and works connected therewith, as they existed on the 1 September 1866, seem to have been deemed sufficient for all purposes, and have been so handed over to this Company to maintain in the future. You are aware that such additional works as have been constructed for this purpose have, in the meantime, by mutual agreement, been paid by this Company, and the interest upon the expenditure charged against the moiety of the surplus traffic, over £27,000 per annum, belonging to the Deeside Company. The Directors of this Company think that the time has now arrived when a proper and permanent arrangement should be come to, under which all such works as are necessary for the proper accommodation of the traffic may be carried out as required, and the necessary powers therefore obtained. They are desirous that such an arrangement should be discussed in the most friendly spirit, and with a view to the mutual advantage of both Companies; and I have now to request that your Board will appoint a small committee to meet with a similar committee of the Board of this Company to initiate the basis of such an arrangement.

Time tends to mellow, and the reasonable terms of the Great North's letter evoked a reasonable response from the Deeside shareholders who were promised that their approval would be sought before any Parliamentary action was undertaken.

Committees were duly appointed by both companies and a report was made to the Deeside Company recommending an amalgamation with the Great North. On Thursday, 17 February 1876, extraordinary general meetings of the three companies concerned were held at the Douglas Hotel in Aberdeen. The Great North approved the proposed Bill unanimously as did the Aboyne & Braemar, which was to be included in the amalgamation. At the Deeside meeting one dissentient voice criticised the way the Great North had been running the Extension line, but with that solitary exception the meeting also approved the proposals. Thus the amalgamation went forward to Parliament with scarcely a ripple raised, in contrast to the storm over the original lease.

'The Great North of Scotland Railway (Further Powers) Act, 1876' received Royal Assent on 13 July of that year. It provided that

> the undertaking of the Deeside Railway Company shall, as and from the thirty-first day of August one thousand eight hundred and seventy-five . . . be amalgamated with and merged in and form part of the Great North of Scotland Railway and that The existing undertaking of the Aboyne & Braemar Railway Company shall, as from the thirty-first day of January one thousand eight hundred and seventy-six . . . be amalgamated with and merged in and form part of the Great North of Scotland Railway.

The agreement was thus retrospective and was potentially a generous one to the Deeside shareholders. The original stock was guaranteed a return of 9¼ per cent in 1876, 9½ per cent in 1877, 9¾ per cent the year after and 10 per cent in 1879, while for the same years the Extension stock was entitled to 6 per cent, £6 3s 9d per cent, £6 6s 3d per cent and 6¼ per cent. The Great North was required to create new stock which, after the maximum dividends mentioned above had been reached, were to be exchanged for the old Deeside stock.

The Great North served the Deeside line well, regarding it as one of its main tourist attractions and giving it more than a fair share of publicity. One small amenity which was introduced in 1918 was the provision of name boards at some of the stations, showing the height above sea level. These were

Banchory	170 ft
Torphins	434 ft
Lumphanan	555 ft
Aboyne	395 ft
Dinnet	530 ft
Ballater	660 ft

Following the 1914-18 war, in common with all railways, difficulties were experienced by the Great North in catching up with long overdue maintenance all over the system. As a result, the Deeside line once again changed hands, but this time at Government insistence as part of the grouping finally effected in 1923. The necessary legislation for this was embodied in the Railway Act, 1921 which received Royal Assent on 19 August.

To ensure equality of treatment, it was decided to split Scotland and England longitudinally, including some Scottish companies with each of the two groups of mainly English concerns. The four new groups were roughly divided by lines radiating from London, the southern part of the country forming the Great Western and Southern Railways, while to the north the two groups were mainly composed of west and east coast lines. The North Western, Midland and West Scottish Group, later to be known as the London, Midland & Scottish Railway, comprised the London & North Western, the Midland, the Lancashire and Yorkshire, the North Staffordshire, the Furness, the **Caledonian**, the **Glasgow & South Western**, and the **Highland** Railways. To the east the North Eastern, Eastern and East Scottish Group, which became the London & North Eastern Railway, comprised the North Eastern, Great Central, Great Eastern, Hull & Barnsley, **North British** and **Great North of Scotland Railways**. Among all the ex-Great railways of the LNE, the Great North of Scotland was the smallest. The names of the Scottish Railways in the two groups have been printed in bold type so that the strategic situation may be more clearly seen.

The GNS was joined with the North British, which came only as far north as Kinnaber Junction, near Montrose, and was thus isolated from it by thirty-eight miles of LMS track over which the LNE had inherited the North British's running powers. The same type of anomaly which placed the West Highland line in the LNE group, surrounded by the LMS, also isolated the Deeside along with the rest of the Great North system, again in LMS territory. This meant that the Great North of Scotland Railway was still surrounded by its old enemies—the erstwhile Highland Railway to the west and Caledonian to the south—and was in the opposite camp once more. The logic of having a totally-isolated system such as the old Great North became, is highly questionable, but this was the arrangement which Parliament in its wisdom made and thus it remained for the next twenty-four years.

This time the Deeside line was only moderately well served by its new master. With control of policy coming from a head office in London, more than 500 miles to the south, one could hardly have expected such intimate touch with the problems and needs of the line as had existed in the days when the Great North of Scotland Railway offices were in Guild Street, just across the road from the line's terminus at the joint station. The LNE was indeed responsible for the first stages of running-down the Deeside line, and also responsible for the first closures on the line. It is true that much was done in the way of track re-laying, provision of Sunday services and so on, but the LNE's financial interest in the competing bus company must have made heavy expenditure on the line seem unreasonable.

In 1939, the country again found itself at war and, as in 1918 so in 1945 the nation's railways emerged sadly run down and in need of modernising. This time there was also a changed political climate and the solution arrived at was nationalisation. The days of the privately-owned railway were numbered. By the 'Transport Act, 1947' which received Royal Assent on 6 August, all British railways were brought together under the *aegis* of a British Transport Commission, as from January 1948.

Under the Railway Executive the country was divided into regions and in this division the Scottish Railways were finally brought together under one administrative control, with the Anglo-Scottish border as its boundary. With direct control centred in Edinburgh it may have seemed that all would be well for such useful and attractive lines as the Deeside, but again there was lacking that spirit of aggression and initiative with which the line had been built and run in independent days. British Railways was responsible for reducing the line as far as Park to single track and despite a number of palliatives the line failed to show a profit. The British Railways Board (which as a result of the 1962 Transport Act had replaced the BTC Railway Executive in an administrative reshuffle) finally implemented the recommendations of the Beeching Report and the line was closed in 1966.

SINGLE-LINE WORKING

The Deeside line was built as a single track throughout and, apart from the section as far as Park, remained such for its whole life. The working of single lines has always posed special problems and the Deeside was a model of its kind with never a serious accident attributable to the way it was worked.

Originally, passing loops were provided at Banchory, Torphins and Aboyne, and these were later augmented by others at Cults and Park. The early working timetables show that trains were also passed at Culter, Crathes and Lumphanan by the expedient of running one train into a siding while the other passed; at Culter it was the up train that was shunted, and at Crathes and Lumphanan the down train. This facility was retained in the working timetables until 1891-2, by which time the track had been doubled as far as Culter and a crossing loop installed at Lumphanan. When the line was returned to single track in the 1950s, Culter and Park became the only two crossing places between Aberdeen and Banchory.

Originally, the signals were extremely crude. At each station with a crossing loop there was a wooden post on the platform carrying a two-arm three-position semaphore signal. The arm to the left of the post referred to the train approaching it. In the horizontal position the signal indicated 'stop', while forty-five degrees to the post indicated 'proceed with caution'. When the arm disappeared within the post in the vertical position this indicated 'all clear'. At night, the position of the arms was shown by a red, green or white light respectively. Distant signals on the same principle were erected in advance of the stations, and these were operated by hand levers beside the loop line or crossing points, *via* a wire.

By 1902, the signals had been altered to conform with the universal system of red/yellow or green. The posts were gradually replaced by the familiar and typically Scottish lattice iron posts. Connected with the points levers of sidings leading to and from the running line were ground disc signals of the two-position type, showing red and white lights, although these were also altered later to red and green. The LNE subsequently installed upper-quadrant signals along the line and replaced the ground disc signals.

Signalboxes were generally of timber construction and where the platform lengths at crossing places were such that the facing points at each end could not be worked from the one box a secondary or minor box was provided. The main box was always situated at the end giving access to the goods sidings, and contained the tablet instruments. Signals were worked from both boxes, with the main box controlling the working of the minor box.

This practice continued until the withdrawal of passenger traffic in 1966, when the signals were removed from Park, Torphins,

SEMAPHORE SIGNALS.

Semaphore Signals— description of. 37. **Semaphore Signals** are constructed with either ONE or TWO Arms for Day Signals, and Coloured Lamps for Night or Foggy weather.

Side of Post on which Signal is made. The Signal is *invariably made* on the **Left Hand** Side of the Post, as seen by the approaching Engine-driver.

All Right. 38. The **All Right** Signal—**go on**—is shown by the Left Hand Side of the Post being clear, the Arm being within the Post, thus:

Or, by a White Light.

39. The **Caution** Signal—**proceed slowly**—is shown by the Arm on the Left Hand Side being raised half way to the horizontal position, thus:

Or, by a Green Light.

Caution.

40. The **Danger** Signal, always to **stop**, is shown by the Arm being raised to the horizontal position, thus, :

Or, by a Red Light.

Danger.

Page from the GNS rule book of 1867, showing signalling instructions

Lumphanan and Dinnet and the down loops at those stations put out of use; the distant signals at Park and Dinnet were left as markers for the level crossings. Thereafter the freight service was operated on the 'one engine in steam' system with a travelling signalman.

Of the many ways in which a single line may be safely worked only three were ever used on the Deeside—the staff, tablet, and 'one engine in steam' systems. In 1864, the line was fitted with Tyer's two-needle electric telegraph system with which the passage of trains between one station and another could be controlled. The instruments between Aberdeen and Banchory cost the company £15 each for those at the terminals and £25 each for those at intermediate stations.

On the section between Banchory and Aboyne a two-position 'block' instrument was used. This showed indications of 'line clear' or 'train on line' and gave a visible reminder of the *status quo* at any particular time. Despite the use of Tyer's improved Needle Signal Instrument, the human element was still the most important factor in ensuring safety on the line. In 1884, this latter instrument was in use at Ferryhill Junction, Cults, Culter, Park, Crathes, Banchory, Torphins, Lumphanan, Aboyne, Dinnet and Ballater. In 1891 further instruments were installed at Ruthrieston and Murtle and in 1893 at Milltimber; the following year the Ruthrieston instrument was transferred to Holburn Street.

As the amount of traffic increased, the need for a more sophisticated control system became increasingly obvious and coincided with the extension of double track to Culter in 1895. Tyer's Train Tablet System was then installed between Culter and Ballater, although between Culter and Park it was only retained until August 1899, when that section was also doubled.

All the signalboxes at intermediate passing points on the line were equipped with two Tyer instruments—one for the section in each direction—and, after removal of the instrument from Culter in 1899, these were to be found at Park, Crathes, Banchory, Torphins, Lumphanan, Aboyne and Dinnet. After the grouping in 1923 the instruments were replaced by a later development, Tyer's key token apparatus, which was basically similar but employed special keys instead of the round tablet. In the 1950s, when the line was reduced to single track and Culter became the first crossing place, the signalbox there was equipped with token apparatus from the former Midland Railway.

SAFETY ON THE LINE

For the whole of its life, the Deeside was one of the safest stretches of line in the country. Indeed, despite a diligent search, the author has been able to trace only three fatal accidents occurring in the 113 years since the line was built, and only one of these involved a passenger; nor were they the result of bad working practice. This is a remarkable record for a line parts of which carried for some years seventy-one trains a day, and most of which was single.

In retrospect, the first recorded accident was more amusing than alarming. The minute books record that, on 27 June 1854, 'an application from Dr Adams of Banchory for a fee from the Company on account of attendance on the man hurt near Mills of Crathes in consequence of his horse having frightened at the train, was acquiesced in'. Dr Adams received one guinea, the first of many that he was to claim from the railway company for various services rendered to its servants and passengers.

The *Aberdeen Journal's* report of the first fatality appeared in the issue of 16 October 1861. William Duncan, aged 10, met with an accident at Lumphanan which proved fatal.

It appears that the boy had been employed during the day in helping to load trucks with stones at the station. The engine having been linked to the wagons, he took hold of one of them, and clung to it after it was in motion. On the wagon coming opposite the loading bank, the poor boy was thrown down among the wheels, and his left arm and both his legs dreadfully smashed. Surgical assistance was obtained, but he survived only about two hours.

The second two fatalities occurred in 1863. On 5 January of that year a Margaret Duncan (uncanny coincidence of surnames) was killed at Glassel when she rushed towards a train that was shunting, apparently under the impression that it was moving off. Tripping over a pile of passengers' luggage she fell under the train, was run over by a wheel, and killed. In the following December an engine cleaner called James Burnett was killed as the result of catching hold of a carriage on a moving train. In April of the same year an engine driver, William Youngson, was apparently killed at Torphins, although no details are known. The company paid for his funeral.

Other accidents occurred from time to time. The only one involving passengers which can be traced took place on Tuesday,

24 January 1871, when the five o'clock down train ran off the rails at Silverstripe sidings near Banchory. Two or three carriages were destroyed and a Mr Berry, hotelkeeper at the Burnett Arms Hotel in Banchory, and a young man named Fraser, a clerk, were 'rather seriously injured, but the other passengers escaped almost unhurt'. A first-class carriage was thrown on its end and one of the third-class carriages was 'entirely opened upon one side'. The cause of the derailment was not clear, but appears to have been due to a fault at the points.

All derailments were not as serious, as was demonstrated as recently as 1951 when, on 3 December, single-line running was resumed between Culter and Park. Unfortunately the habit of years was deeply ingrained and the 8.11 am train to Ballater was diverted to the newly-closed down line at Culter where it collided with a temporary buffer stop, derailing the B1 class engine and the leading bogie of the first coach. Fortunately no one was hurt.

Undoubtedly other minor accidents occurred on the line, but it is a measure of its excellent safety record that these were so few and so slight as to have gone almost unrecorded.

Page 73 : GNS TRAINS

(24) *No 101 on a down Deeside Express* circa 1910
(25) *Up King's Messenger train on Dinnet Muir*
(26) *The Deeside Express near Cambus O'May*

Page 74 : NEAR ABERDEEN

(27) *In the snow, near Murtle*, 1905
(28) *'Subby' train leaving Cults*
(29) *Down train leaving Culter*

CHAPTER 4

Train Services

When the Deeside line was first opened in September, 1853, it had been intended that an arrangement would be made for the Aberdeen Railway to run the line, but it was in fact the Scottish Central Railway (using the joint stock of its own, the Scottish Midland Junction and the Aberdeen Railways) that provided the trains. The first timetable showed three trains a day in each direction on weekdays only, so arranged that the whole service could be worked by one train. Exactly one hour was taken for the sixteen-mile journey, with stops at each of the five intermediate stations.

It was not long before the arrangement for provision of stock by other companies was found to be unsatisfactory. At the company's second annual meeting on 26 October 1853, only seven weeks after the opening of the line to traffic, the Chairman, John Duncan, reported that the arrangement whereby the Scottish Central Railway agreed 'for a consideration, according to mileage, to supply the line (the Deeside) with locomotive power, and the necessary carriages for passengers and trucks for goods' was not satisfactory and 'could not be carried out with advantage to the company'. Two locomotives had accordingly been ordered by the directors, and about thirty goods wagons purchased. The transit of goods had in fact been a sadly-underestimated side of the traffic.

Initially, there were no proper arrangements for this side of the business, and the line had opened with neither trucks nor goods sheds. The traffic had appeared, however, and arrangements were speedily made to cope with it.

From the beginning there was no second-class, but only 1st and 3rd—a peculiarity common to all railways in north-east Scotland.

Return tickets were issued daily for all trains at one and a half times the ordinary fare, for return on the day of issue only. From 1 October to the 28th in the first year of operation a special cheap train was run on Saturdays, leaving Aberdeen at 3 pm and return-

E

ing from Banchory 'about 8.15 pm'. Tickets issued for this train were valid for return only by it, and not on any other train, the return fares being 1s 6d first-class and 1s third-class. As this was even less than the ordinary single fare, it is not surprising that this train lasted for only four weeks. From the following year (1854) a through booking to Kincardine O'Neil, Aboyne and Ballater was offered, by way of the railway to Banchory and the *Victoria* and *Marquis of Huntly* coaches beyond.

After 1 June, a fourth train each way was added to the timetable and some speeding-up resulted in one train each way doing the journey in 45 min, and all the others (except the first and third up trains) taking 50 or 55 min. In June 1855, the number of trains went up to five each way, although it returned to four for the winter months. In 1856, special goods trains were provided for the first time.

When the Extension Railway was opened in 1859 the first, second and fourth down trains and the second, third and fourth up trains ran through to and from Aboyne, the journey time varying with different trains between 2 and $2\frac{1}{2}$ hr. The following summer, from 2 June (1860), the number of trains in each direction was increased to six, of which four ran through to and from Aboyne, although the service was reduced again for the winter months. For several years thereafter the service did not exceed five trains each way.

When the Aboyne & Braemar Railway opened in 1866, it was stipulated that there should be not less than two trains a day each way between Aboyne and Ballater for eight months of the year, and not less than three each way for the remaining four months. The service was actually begun with three through trains in each direction between Aberdeen and Ballater, while there was also another one to and from Aboyne and another going only as far as Banchory. Most of the trains stopped at each of the fifteen inter-mediate stations and it is not surprising that they took between $2\frac{1}{4}$ and $2\frac{1}{2}$ hr for the $43\frac{1}{4}$ mile journey.

In May 1880, the first real attempt was made at speeding up the services, the 4.30 pm down and the 8.08 am up trains being known as the 'Deeside Express'. This 'express' service cut the time to Ballater to $1\frac{1}{2}$ hr—an average of 28 mph—and had only four inter-mediate stops, but it was notable in a time when nearly all trains in northern Scotland stopped at every station and averaged only 20 mph overall. By the winter of 1884, the service consisted of six passenger and two goods trains leaving Aberdeen each week-

Deeside Section.

UP TRAINS—BALLATER TO ABERDEEN.

	COACHES.									Sun.
	Braemar ___ de.			a.m. 4 45						
	Ballater ___ ar.			4 45						
	Tarland ___ de.									
	Aboyne ___ ar.			*6 45 7 45						

Miles	STATIONS.	1 Mixed 1 & 2	2 Pass. 1 & 2	3 Pass. 1st Class.	4 Pass. 1 & 2	5 Goods.	6 Mixed	7 Pass. 1 & 2	1st Class only.
	Ballater ___ de.	a.m. 7 25	a.m. 7 30	a.m. 9 10	p.m. 10	p.m.	p.m.	a.m. 7 20	a.m. 10 25
6½	Dinnet	7 35	7 44		1 25			7 35	
11	Aboyne {ar. {de.	7 48 7 54	7 53 7 56	9 41	1 39 1 45	2 30		7 46 7 51	
14	Dess	8 5	8 4		1 52	2 45	4 53	8 1	
16½	Lumphanan {ar.	8 20 8 29	8 14		2 58	2 58	6 1	8 11	
19½	Torphins {ar. {de.	8 39	8 26 8 34		2 20 2 29	3 15 3 30	6 1	8 24 8 33	
22	Glassel {ar.	9 0	8 48		2 40	3 50		8 43	
26	Banchory {de.		8 51	10 29	2 45	4 14	6 45	8 50	11 30
29½	Crathes		8 59		2 53	4 31		8 58	
32½	Park		9 9		3 4	4 38		9 1	
33½	Drum		9 12	10 46½	4 4	4 47	6 14	9 10	
35½	Culter {ar. {de.	9 20 9 29	9 19 9 27		3 20 3 31	5 22 5 31		9 19 9 28	
37	Milltimber	8 39					6 32	9 23	
38½	Murtle						6 30	9 36	
38½	Culls								
41½	Ruthrieston								
42½	Aberdeen ___ ar.	9 0	9 50	11 10	3 40	5 55	6 45	9 50	12 5p

	Trains leave	a.m.	p.m.	p.m.	p.m.		p.m.	a.m.	p.m.
	Aberdeen	10 0	1 55		4 43		7 0	8 30	12 23
	Peterhead	12 15	4 30		5 35		8 0	10 55	6 15
	Fraserburgh ___ ar.	12 56	4 35		6 25		9 10	11 20	6 20
	Aberdeen ___ de.	10 0	1 20		4 43			8 30	
	Alford	12 15		2 10	5 35			10 55	
	Inverurie	10 56			5 25			11 20	
	Oldmeldrum				8 5				
	Macduff	2 15p		4 0	7 20		10 30		
	Portsoy	12 50		5 57	7 20		12 30		
	Keith	2 40		5 40	9 20		11 5		
	Elgin								
	Trains leave	p.m.		p.m.	p.m.		p.m.	p.m.	
	Aberdeen, per Cal.	9 20	12 23		4 15		12 23	6 0	
	Glasgow	4 23	6 15		9 45		6 15	1 0p	
	Edinburgh, per Cal.	4 28	6 20		9 45		6 20	1 0	
	Do. per N.B.	3 49	7 0		9 45		7 0	7 0	
	London, via G. N.								
	Do. via L. & N.W.	6 0	4 37d		9 40		4 37d	4 40d	

* On Mondays, Tuesdays, and Saturdays only.

† Stop at Drum by Signal when Passengers are to be taken on. Passengers are not to be booked or carried to Drum by this Train.

‡ On Mondays, Fridays, and Saturday only. Passengers not to be carried to or from Culter by this Train.

NOTE.—A line across the column denotes the Stations appointed for the Trains to meet and pass each other; and in no case shall a Train passing in one direction leave the Station where a Train coming in an opposite direction has to pass, till this Train has arrived and passed into the Station clear of the Points.

DOWN TRAINS—ABERDEEN TO BALLATER.

	Trains leave					p.m.		p.m.
	London, via G. N.	a.m. 10 0				8 40		9 15
	Do. via L. & N.W.	10 0				6 40a		9 15
	Glasgow	9 0p				6 25		9 35a
	Edinburgh, via Cal.	8 45				6 25		9 45
	Do. via N. B.	3 0a				12 35p		4 15p

Miles	STATIONS.	1 Pass. 1st Class.	2 Pass. 4 Mill 1 & 3.	3 Goods	4 Pass. 1 & 3	5 Mixed 1 & 3.	6 Pass. 1 & 3	7 Pass. 1 & 3	Sun. 1st Class only.
	Aberdeen ___ de.	a.m. 3 10	a.m. 7 45	a.m. 10 0	a.m. 11 30	p.m. 2 40	p.m. 4 35	p.m. 7 20	p.m. 12 40
2	Ruthrieston			10 3					
3½	Culls		8 6	10 23		2 58		7 45	
5½	Murtle		8 9	10 38	11 46	3 7	4 55	7 49	
6½	Milltimber		8 22	10 40	11 51	3 15		7 43	
7½	Culter {ar. {de.	8 13	8 13	10 51	11 58	3 28	5 11	5 47	
10	Drum		8 27	11 1	12 9	3 26	5 19	7 57	
11	Park		8 37	11 22	12 24	3 40	5 30	8 12	
14	Crathes		8 45	11 32	12 33	3 51	5 39	8 20	
17	Banchory {ar. {de.		9 2	12 0	12 37	3 55	5 42		1 25
21½	Glassel {ar.	3 55	9 10	12 15	12 56	5 58	5 58		
24	Torphins {ar. {de.		9 22	12 31	1 6p	1 22	6 21		
27	Lumphanan {ar. {de.		9 30	12 44	1 32		6 30		
29½	Dess		9 51	1 Out.	1 52	1 58	6 40		
32½	Aboyne		10 0		2 0	2 10	5 51	6	
37	Dinnet								
43½	Ballater ___ ar.	5			2 30	5 0			
	COACHES.								
	Aboyne ___ de.		10 25				*6 45		2 30
	Tarland ___ ar.		12 45						
	Ballater ___ de.								
	Braemar ___ ar.								

Not worked on Mondays.

day, half of them stopping at Banchory and the other half working right through to Ballater. The passenger trains still took about three-quarters of an hour to reach Banchory but only around two hours to get all the way to Ballater.

At this time a special platform existed near Craigmyle House at Torphins for the benefit of the occupants. The working time-tables stipulated that 'Ordinary (but not Express) Trains may stop at Craigmyle by request of Mr Gordon or other Resident or Visitor at Craigmyle House, for the purpose of setting down or taking up Passengers'.

By the spring of 1891, the need for a local service was being felt and a Saturdays-only train was running as far as Culter, taking 20 min, while the traffic from upper Deeside had also increased sufficiently for four of the six regular passenger trains to run through to Ballater. In November of the same year, five of the trains began to run through, and the journey time was cut to 1¼ hr.

Traffic continued to increase and extra trains were put on during the following summers to Banchory and a Saturdays-only to Cults, which took ten minutes (only two minutes outside British Railways' standard time when the line closed). The Banchory goods train was also extended to run through to Ballater.

It was in July 1894 that a real suburban service was begun between Aberdeen and Culter, following the pattern established on the other side of the city between Aberdeen and Dyce seven years earlier. Commencement of the Deeside suburban service had been held up by the lack of a double track but when, in the summer of 1894, this was extended to Culter a service of ten down and nine up trains daily on weekdays was begun. Timing was very smart, twenty-one minutes being allowed for the down journey and twenty-two for the up, with seven intermediate stops in the 7¼ miles. Although an eighth stop was added in 1897 (at Bieldside) the timing remained virtually unaltered until the service was with-drawn forty-three years later in the April of 1937. Known locally as the 'Subbies', these trains provided the only suburban service in Scotland outside Edinburgh and Glasgow, but were eventually superseded by buses. The number of trains on this service soon increased and within ten years had reached nineteen in each direction daily.

In considering the 'subby' service we have jumped on several years, but the main-line service did not alter very much in this time, although most of the Ballater trains no longer stopped at the stations between Aberdeen and Culter except to set down passengers travelling through from the south and to pick up those going west of Culter. The up Ballater trains generally stopped at Holburn Street for 'Collection and Examination of Tickets' and passengers on these trains could be booked to alight there, although it was not a scheduled stop in the timetable. A few up express trains did not stop at all between Banchory and the joint station, and tickets of Aberdeen passengers on these trains were collected at Banchory and sent to Holburn Street by the next train.

In 1907 an arrangement was begun whereby the 6.45 pm up 'subby' train ran on to Schoolhill station. This platform was within sight of the joint station and was the first suburban station on the Dyce route. As it was adjacent to the theatre this was a convenience much appreciated by the suburban passengers having a night out, especially as they were not charged any extra for the ⅜ mile journey.

Later in the evening the 10.33 pm train from Dyce worked right through to Culter as the 10.55 pm Deeside down train, thus providing a convenient return service from Schoolhill. This through service continued until 1917.

Goods trains in the Great North days usually served only Cults and Murtle to the east of Culter, although beyond Culter nearly every station was served regularly except Drum and Cambus O'May, where a service more or less 'as required' was in force. For many years the working timetables contained a note relating to some down freight trains that read: 'stops at Cambus O'May with Gunpowder when required'. This service was for the nearby granite quarries.

The year 1914 saw the period of the greatest amount of traffic on the line—there were six passenger, one express and two goods trains a day running through in each direction to Ballater plus an extra passenger train on Wednesdays and Saturdays only, as well as four local trains to Banchory running each day and two more passenger trains on a Wednesday and Saturday. There were also eighteen 'subby' trains and one goods to Culter. A third passenger 'Saturday only' train ran down to Banchory during July and August so that on Saturdays Culter saw thirty-six down and thirty-five up trains during those months—seventy-one trains during the day, the zenith of rail traffic on Deeside.

In 1914 there was also an unusual experiment with a slip-coach to Banchory. Slip-coaches were never widely used in Scotland. The Great North service was however quite unique in being the only

DOWN TRAINS.   Deeside Section.

Trains leave	a.m.	a.m.	p.m.	p.m.	p.m.	a.m.		p.m.	p.m.				p.m.	p.m.		
London (Euston)	10 0		2 0		s8 0			9 15	9 15					10 0		
Do. (St Pancras)		10 30	10s30													
Do. (King's Cross)		10 35		s9 0				8 30					10s40			
Do. (Liverpool Street)		8 45		s9 52												
Edin. (v. Stirling & Dunblane)			9 45p			4 45		6 45a					9 40a			
Do. (v. Forth and Tay Bridges, and Montrose)		9 0p		4 33a				7 15a					9 35a			
Glasgow (Buchanan Street)	6 20p		10 0			8c10			7 15				10 0			
Do. (Queen St.) r. Tay Bridge		8 10						5 55					9 0			
Perth	5 5		12s32		1s45	7 0			9 15				11 40			
Aberdeen _____arrive	10 15	12s30	3 7	7 35	7s50	9 0		11 0	12p10				1 35p	2 5p		
Trains leave					a.m.			a.m.	a.m.							
Inverness	3 45							6 0	8 45							10 10
Elgin v. Buckie	5 45							6 40	10 20							10 40
Do. v. Craigellachie	6 5							7 15	9 40							11 40
Keith	7 30				6 10			8 35	11 20							12 55
Buckie	6 23							7 16	10 47							11 20
Macduff						6 0		9 0								12 16
Oldmeldrum						7 5		10 0								1 35
Inverurie	8 50					7 45		10 15								2 25
Alford						7 5		9 15								1 40
Aberdeen _____arrive	9 30					8 30		11 0		12 55p						3 13
Fraserburgh _____depart	7 0				7 0			5 25								12 55
Peterhead _____	7 10				7 15			9 28								1 0
Aberdeen _____arrive	9 10				9 20			11 30								3 20

	1	2	3	4	5	6	7	8	9	10	11	12	13	14	15	16
STATIONS	Not on Mons. Queen's Special	Pass. 1, 3.	Pass. 1, 3.	Pass 1, 3.	Pass. 1, 3. and Mail.	Goods	Pass. 1, 3.	Fast. 1, 3.	Fast. 1, 3.	Pass. 1, 3.			Pass. 1, 3.	Pass. 1, 3.	Goods	Pass. 1, 3.
	a.m.	a.m.	a.m.	a.m.	a.m.	a.m.	a.m.	p.m.	p.m.	p.m.			p.m.	p.m.	p.m.	a.m.
ABERDEEN _____depart	†3 30	6 30	7 45	8 5	9 30	9 33	10 15	12 5	12 25	1 5			2 55	3 10	3 13	4 15
Holburn Street		6 33	7 48				10 18	12 8		1 8			2 58			4 18
Ruthrieston		6 35	7 50				10 20	12 10		1 10			3 0			4 20
Pitfodels		6 38	7 53				10 23	12 13		1 13			3 3			4 23
Cults		6 40	7 55		9 38	9 53	10 25	12 15		1 15			3 5			4 25
West Cults		6 42	7 57				10 27	12 17		1 17			3 7			4 27
Murtle		6 45	8 0		9 42	10 3	10 30	12 20		1 20			3 10		§	4 30
Milltimber		6 48	8 3		9 45	10 11	10 33	12 23		1 23			3 13			4 33
Culter _____arrive		6 51	8 6				10 36	12 26		1 26			3 16			4 36
Do. _____depart				8 19	9 48	10 25			12 39					3 24	3 46	
Drum				8 25	9 54	10 37			12 45					3 30		
Park				8 28	9 57	10 45			12 48					3 33	4 0	
Crathes				8 34	10 3	10 58			12 55					3 39	4 10	
Banchory _____arrive				8 40	10 9	11 8			1 1					3 45	4 20	
Do. _____depart				8 43	10 12	11 18			1 5					3 48	5 0	
Glassel				8 53	10 22	11 35			1 16					3 58	5 20	
Torphins				9 0	10 27	11 47			1 22					4 3	5 33	
Lumphanan				9 8	10 34	12p2			1 31					4 11	5 49	
Dess				9 13	10 39	12 12			1 37					4 16	5 59	
Aboyne _____arrive				9 20	10 46	12 29			1 45					4 25	6 15	
Do. _____depart				9 30	10 55	12 45			1 55					4 35	6 34	
Dinnet				9 36	11 1	12 55			2 1					4 41		
Cambus O'May				9 45	11 10	1 13			2 10					4 50	6 50	
BALLATER _____arrive	5 0															

§ Stops at Murtle with draff when required.   d Stops for Crossing purposes only.
j Stops at Cambus o' May with Gunpowder when required.   † Stops where required to set down Passengers off South Train.

General Notes applicable to Working the Trains.

CRATHES BALLAST SIDING.—Points facing Up Trains connect this Siding with Main Line. The Points will be kept locked and all right for Trains passing; they will only be opened for Ballasting purposes by Way Inspector, who will be responsible for the Points being locked and all right for the Trains. Drivers and Guards are to be cautious in passing the Ballast Siding.

SILVERSTRIPE SIDING, BANCHORY.—This Siding is worked in connexion with Banchory Station. 7·55 a.m. Up and 3·13 p.m. Down Trains to work the traffic. Agent at Banchory is responsible that the Points which face Down Trains are kept locked and all clear for Trains passing.

Train Crossing Stations.

DOWN TRAINS.

No. 4 Down 8·5 a.m. Train crosses 7·55 a.m. Up Banchory Train at Culter, 7·40 a.m. Up Train at Banchory, and 7·55 a.m. Up Goods Train at Torphins.

No. 5 Down 9·30 a.m. Train crosses 7·55 a.m. Up Goods Train at Park, and 10·20 a.m. Up Train at Aboyne.

No. 6 Down 9·33 a.m. Goods Train crosses 7·55 a.m. Up Goods Train at Culter, 10·20 a.m. Up Train at Banchory, and 12·8 p.m. Up Train at Aboyne.

No. 9 Down 12·25 p.m. Train crosses 12·5 p.m. Up Train at Banchory, and 1·35 p.m. Up Goods Train at Dinnet.

No. 14 Down 3·10 p.m. Train crosses 1·35 p.m. Up Goods Train at Banchory, 3·30 p.m. Up Train at Lumphanan, and 4·5 p.m. Up Express Train at Aboyne.

No. 15 Down 3·13 p.m. Goods Train crosses 1·35 p.m. Up Goods Train at Crathes, both 3·30 p.m. and 4·5 p.m. Up Trains at Banchory, and 6·20 p.m. Up Train at Dinnet.

No. 19 Down 5·35 p.m. Train crosses 6·20 p.m. Up Train at Aboyne.

No. 22 Down 7·30 p.m. Train crosses 6·20 p.m. Up Train at Culter.

Pages from the GNS working ti

Trains leave	p.m.		p.m.	night				a.m.	a.m.	p.m.	p.m.
London (Euston)				12 0				5 15		2 0	8 50
Do. (St. Pancras)										10,30	9 15
Do. (King's Cross)									10 0		8 30
Do. (Liverpool Street)									5 45		
Edin. (v. Stirling & Dumblane)				1 35p				4 30p		9,45	6.35
Do. (v. Forth and Tay Bridges, and Montrose			1 50						6 40p		7 0
Glasgow (Buchanan Street)				2 0				5 0		10 0	6c15
Do. (Queen St.) r. Tay Bridge			1 20						5 35		6 10
Perth	12 5			4 0				6 55		12.32	8 30
Aberdeen _____arrive	3 52		6 0	6 30				9 5	10 5	3 7	11 0
Trains leave			p.m.			p.m.		p.m.			
Inverness			12 40			3 0		3 45			
Elgin v. Buckie			2 26			3 0		5 45			
Do. v. Craigellachie			2 25					6 5			
Keith			3 20			5 0		7 20			
Buckie			2 52			3 52		6 23			
Macduff			2 15			4 0					
Oldmeldrum			3 58			5 25					
Inverurie			4 42			6 14		8 50			
Alford						5 10					
Aberdeen _____arrive			5 14			6 45		9 30			
			p.m								
Fraserburgh _____depart			3 35					7 0			
Peterhead			3 40					7 10			
Aberdeen			5 20					9 10			

	17	18	19	20	21	22	23	24	25		
STATIONS.										SUNDAYS	
										Queen's Speci.	Exp. Pass. 1,2.
		Pass. 1,3.	Pass. 1,3.	Pass. 1 & 3.		Pass. 1,3.	Pass. 1,3.	Pass. 1,3.		a.m.	p.m.
ABERDEEN _____depart		p.m. 5 5	p.m. 5 35	p.m. 6 15		p.m. 7 30	p.m. 9 0	p.m. 10 30		†8 30	12†30
Holburn Street		5 9		6 18		7 34	9 3	10 33			
Ruthrieston		5 11		6 20		7 36	9 5	10 35			
Pitfodels		5 14		6 23		7 39	9 8	10 38			
Cults		5 16		6 25		7 41	9 10	10 40			
West Cults		5 18		6 27		7 43	9 12	10 42			
Murtle		5 22		6 30		7 47	9 15	10 45			
Milltimber		5 25		6 33		7 50	9 18	10 48			
Culter _____arrive		5 28		6 36			9 21	10 51			
Do. _____depart			5 48			7 54					
Drum			5 54			8 0					
Park			5 57			8 3					
Crathes			6 3			8 9					
Banchory _____arrive			6 9			8 15					1 3
Do. _____depart			6 12								1 5
Glassel			6 21								
Torphins			6 26								
Lumphanan			6 34								
Dess			6 39								
Aboyne _____arrive			6 45								
Do. _____depart			6 46								1 56
Dinnet			6 56								
Cambus O'May			7 2								
BALLATER _____arrive			7 10							5 0	2 0

Train Crossing Stations.

UP TRAINS.

No. 4 Up 7·40 a.m. Train crosses 8·5 a.m. Down Train at Banchory.

No. 6 Up 7·55 a.m. Goods Train crosses 8·5 a.m. Down Train at Torphins and 9·30 a.m. Down Train at Park.

No. 8 Up 10·20 a.m. Train crosses 9·30 a.m. Down Train at Aboyne, and 9·33 a.m. Down Goods Train at Banchory.

No. 10 Up 12·5 p.m. Train crosses 9·33 a.m. Down Goods Train at Aboyne and 12·25 p.m. Down Train at Banchory.

No. 14 Up 3·20 p.m. Train crosses 3·10 p.m. Down Train at Lumphanan, 3·13 p.m. Down Goods Train at Banchory, and passes 1·35 p.m. Up Goods Train at Culter.

No. 15 Up 4·5 p.m. Express Train crosses 3·10 p.m. Down Train at Aboyne, 3·13 p.m. Down Goods Train at Banchory, and passes 1·35 p.m. Up Goods Train at Culter.

No. 17 Up 1·35 p.m. Goods Train crosses 12·25 p.m. Down Train at Dinnet, 3·10 p.m. Down Train at Banchory, 3·13 p.m. Down Goods Train at Crathes, and shunts at Culter to allow both 3·30 p.m. and 4·5 p.m. Up Trains to pass and go before it.

No. 22 Up 6·20 p.m. Train crosses 3·13 p.m. Down Goods Train at Dinnet, and 5·35 p.m. Down Train at Aboyne.

showing the first suburban service

slip-coach ever operated on a standard-gauge single-line route. The slip service was the outcome of an arrangement whereby express trains were no longer required to stop at Crathes, and in consequence the 4.45 pm down express was speeded up to do the journey from Aberdeen to Ballater in 1 hr 15 min, calling only at Torphins and Aboyne *en route*, and slipping one or more coaches at Banchory.

The working timetable for June 1914 shows the train passing Banchory at 5.07 pm, and 'the Slip-Coaches will be due to arrive Banchory at 5.8 pm'. The reference to slip-coaches in the plural is interesting as it is believed that only one coach was ever equipped for slipping. The slipped coach was picked up by the 8.30 am up express the following day. The experiment never really had a chance to get off the ground, as the outbreak of war caused the service to be withdrawn after only two months, and it was never restored.

The Deeside Express itself continued to appear in the timetable after the war until the outbreak of the 1939 war, when it was finally discontinued.

During the 1914-18 war the Deeside services were only slightly reduced, the 'subby' service remaining unaltered while the number of trains to and from Banchory was reduced by only one. The through service to Ballater was the most affected, losing two ordinary passenger trains a day as well as the express. The whole line also lost its Wednesday and Saturday only trains and after the war neither these nor the other cut trains were replaced, apart from the express, which was restored in 1920.

Following grouping in 1923, the LNE made virtually no changes for the first few years, but in 1928 Sunday services were introduced as from 1 June. With a weekday service of nineteen trains to and from Culter, four more to Banchory (plus one on Saturdays only) and five more to Ballater, the Sunday service, beginning at 1.30 pm from Aberdeen and 2.05 pm from Culter, provided an hourly suburban service with nine trains to and from Culter, in addition to three more trains each way to and from Banchory and one right through to Ballater. Through the following winter the Sunday service was slightly curtailed to eight each way as far as Culter, and in 1929 the service to Culter was increased to a half-hourly frequency with the introduction of the Sentinel-Cammell steam railcar, so that on Sundays there were sixteen trains to and from Culter, four for Banchory and another to Ballater.

During the winter of 1929-30 the Culter service remained unaltered, only the Banchory and Ballater trains being taken off, and being replaced again in the spring. Pressure from competing bus services was intense and Scots are inclined to be conservative about travel on the Sabbath, so the Sunday suburban services came to an abrupt end with the introduction of the winter timetable in September 1930. Sunday trains continued to run to Banchory and Ballater in the summer months and in June 1934 the Sunday 'subbies' were resurrected for three more summers only, but in September 1936 they were finally withdrawn, only a few months before the weekday service was also withdrawn as and from 5 April 1937. The Sunday trains to Banchory and Ballater continued to run until 1939 when the advent of war caused their final disappearance.

During the war the Deeside service suffered along with all other rail services, and there were only four trains a day in each direction, summer and winter. Freight services were considerably augmented however, to carry much-needed timber from the Deeside forests to Aberdeen for distribution. The loads carried rose from 46,000 tons in 1940 to 177,000 tons in 1943. It was stated that between 1940-44 the line carried 539,000 tons of sawn timber, pit-props and pulpwood for paper, using 120,000 wagons and an average of six times the normal number of trains.

After the war the passenger service became even worse, the last LNE timetable before nationalisation showing only three trains to and from Ballater each day and one extra on Saturdays only. British Railways gradually built up this service, with four trains a day in the winter of 1947, and in ensuing summers an additional Saturdays only train also, although the winter service fell back to three trains a day.

THE LAST GREAT OCCASION

On Wednesday, 26 March 1958 there occurred the last great 'opening' on the line. British Railways was introducing to Deeside the first battery electric railcar in Britain. With battery charging at off-peak rates, it was expected that great economies would be effected, as well as an increase in traffic ensuing. The first run of the railcar was a private showing to 117 selected guests.

There was snow on the ground as the car pulled out of Ballater at 4.21 pm to the cheers of the crowd and the skirl of pipes. 'It was a historic day for Royal Deeside, which is to have this newest, cheapest, cleanest and most silent form of rail transport' stated *The*

Scotsman the next day and 'this streamlined form of transport . . . should woo back thousands of travellers from the roads'. The Aberdeen *Press and Journal* agreed, stating that 'A new era in British railway travel was inaugurated' and describing the 'gala occasion' with 'hundreds of spectators' and 'cheers all along the route'. Little could they foresee that this would be virtually the last fling in an attempt to regain lost custom and that less than eight years later passenger services would be withdrawn completely.

When the train arrived at Aberdeen sixty-six minutes later there was a crowd behind the barriers to greet it. It was nearly a month later, on Monday 21 April—the Aberdeen Spring Holiday— that the first public run took place, the railcar leaving Aberdeen at 9.40 am with every seat occupied. The battery car was based at Ballater and made three runs in each direction daily 'until it was eventually replaced by a diesel multiple-unit' running alternately with a two-car diesel multiple-unit, steam trains being withdrawn from the branch from that time on.

With the introduction of the battery-electric railcar and diesel multiple-units, the service was augmented to six trains daily in each direction in summer and five in winter, and at this level it remained until the withdrawal of passenger services in February 1966.

A freight service continued to run, although this was curtailed. Latterly the service had consisted of one train to and from Ballater each Monday, Wednesday and Friday and another to and from Culter on Tuesday and Thursday, this last service being withdrawn at the same time as the passenger service. The freight service was not destined to be long-lived. On Friday, 15 July 1966 the last train ran from Ballater, the service becoming Monday, Wednesday and Friday to Culter, as required. Even this limited service soon ceased and, on Friday, 30 December, the last train on Deeside— an assortment of timber and brakevans—saw the end of travel on the Deeside Line.

THE MESSENGERS

The Messenger trains comprised yet another feature of the Deeside railway that was unique. When Queen Victoria began to spend part of each year at Balmoral it became the practice for her despatches to be brought daily by train as far as Perth, and then by pony and trap by way of Blairgowrie, Cairnwell and Braemar, a journey of sixty miles or thereabouts coming over the Devil's

Elbow and involving a climb to over 2,000 ft above sea level.

As the Queen herself was using the Deeside Raiway to travel to and from her Highland home it occurred to the company that there was no reason why her messengers should not do likewise and, in 1864, the secretary wrote to General Grey, the Queen's private secretary, proposing the provision of special trains to connect with those running between London and Aberdeen, and the supply of a carriage between the company's terminus at Aboyne and Balmoral Castle. An agreement was eventually reached with the Home Office that for the sum of £9 2s 0d per day a train would be provided in each direction as far as Aboyne, and a carriage and pair to complete the journey.

The service commenced on 8 October 1865 with a down train leaving Aberdeen at 4.00 am, and, stopping only at Banchory, reaching Aboyne at 5.25 am. For the return journey the up messenger left Aboyne at 2.15 pm, and arrived at Aberdeen at 3.33 pm, having also stopped only at Banchory. When in 1866 the line was opened to Ballater, the service was extended there, the down train arriving at 5.50 am. There was no up train at this stage, the courier presumably travelling on the ordinary 1.35 pm train which arrived at Aberdeen at 3.40 pm, although in 1868 there was an up messenger train leaving Ballater at 2.10 and taking an hour and fifty minutes to reach Aberdeen.

It appears that the company was hard-pressed for motive power to run the extra trains and so approaches were made to the Great North for the loan of an engine to tide it over. The Great North offered an old tender engine for hire at 6d per train-mile for one month only but, as this engine would not fit the Aboyne turntable, the offer was not taken up. (Minutes of Traffic & Finance Committee September 20, 1865.)

It is said that the early messenger trains were very colourful affairs, with engines painted tartan and the single coaches in purple and gold with the royal cipher on their sides. Although the contract was a definite piece of prestige for the company, it is certain that the trains were not run for profit, for the £9 fee for each even included the courier's breakfast.

Initially, each train consisted of a solitary coach for the messenger and his despatches, but later a second coach was added to accommodate VIPs *en route* to visit the Queen. Subsequently a first-class public coach was also included, and passengers' servants permitted to travel at third-class fares.

The early messenger trains ran on weekdays only, except

Mondays, but in 1870 the Post Office subsidised a Sunday train to provide a collection and delivery of mail during the Queen's stay at Balmoral; this train left Ballater in the morning and returned from Aberdeen in the early afternoon. In 1871 the railway began to use this service as a Sunday messenger train.

Complaints were often made in the early days that the messenger arrived late at Ballater station from Balmoral, thus delaying the train, and in 1880 the up train was scheduled to depart five minutes later, and the following year put back another fifty minutes to 3.05 pm, arriving at Aberdeen at 4.30 pm. By this time there were two down trains on Sundays, leaving Aberdeen at 3.30 am and 1 pm and arriving at Ballater at 5.15 am and 2.50 pm respectively. In 1882 the down morning train ceased to stop regularly at Banchory and Aboyne and stopped only by request to set down passengers from the south at any station. It arrived at Ballater at 5 am, and this timing was retained until the 1914-18 war when, as the King did not go to Balmoral, the service was broken. After the war the timing was altered to 3.55 am from Aberdeen, arriving at Ballater at 5.10 am, and later again to 3.45 am, arriving 5 am.

By the turn of the century the up afternoon train had been put back even further and eventually left Ballater at 4.15 pm before the war, arriving at Aberdeen at 5.30 pm to connect with the 5.45 pm west-coast train to the south.

Because of the early hour of the morning down messengers, special arrangements were made with regard to signalling. For many years, up until the first war, the working timetables specified that these trains, and the 12.30 pm Sunday express,

> are to be worked without being signalled from station to station; but Ballater must Telegraph the arrival of the 3.30 am Down Train to Aberdeen at 7.40 am, and the 8.0 am Down Train is not to leave Aberdeen until this report is received.

After the war the regulations became more complex.

> The 3.55 am Down (Week-days and Sundays) Train is *not* to be signalled on the Block Telegraph and Train Tablet Instruments from Ferryhill Junction to Aboyne, but must be signalled on Train Tablet Instruments from Aboyne to Ballater, except on Sundays when it will not be signalled throughout to Ballater. It must, however, get the proper fixed signals from Aberdeen to Ballater.

On weekdays, no down Deeside train was allowed to leave Aberdeen until the 3.55 was notified as having passed Park, nor 'until receipt of the latter advice must a Down Train leave Park or an Up Train leave Banchory'. Other complicated arrangements existed for Sundays.

GREAT NORTH OF SCOTLAND RAILWAY.

SUPPLEMENT TO
WORKING TIME TABLES,
FOR THE
GUIDANCE OF THE COMPANY'S OFFICERS AND SERVANTS ONLY.

From 1st October, 1912, & until His Majesty leaves Balmoral.

DEESIDE SECTION.

Additional and Altered Trains will be run as follows, until further notice.—

DOWN TRAINS.	Week-days.				Sundays.		UP TRAINS.	Week-days.		Sun-days.	
	Not Mons Pass.	Express Pass.	2·50 p.m. Goods altered from Banch'ry	Ety. Carrs.	Pass.	Pass.		Express Pass.	6·35 a.m. Goods altered from Banchory	Pass.	Pass.
	A.M.	P.M.	P.M.	P.M.	A.M.	P.M.		A.M.	A.M.	P.M.	P.M.
Aberd'n, de	3†30	4 35	...	6 40	3†30	12†20	Ballater, de.	8 30	...	4 15	2 0
Culter .	...	4 47	...	6 53	...	...	Dinnet .	...	...	...	•
Drum .	...	4 52	...	...	...	...	Aboyne .	8 45	...	4 36	2 17
Park . .	...	5 55	...	7 1	...	...	Torphins .	9 0	...	4 50	...
Crathes .	...	5 1	...	...	...	...	Banchory .	9T11	9 17	5 T 5	2T45
Banchory .	...	5 6	5 20	7 15	...	12 46	Crathes .	9e16	9 39	5 e10	...
Torphins .	...	5 19	5 40	Stop	...	...	Park . .	...	9 54	...	...
Lumph'nan	...	...	5 55	...	...	...	Drum .	...	10 3	...	...
Aboyne .	...	5T34	6 11	...	...	1 12	Culter, arr.	...	10 11	...	...
Dinnet .	...	...	6 29	...	...	...	Culter, dep.	9e26	10 31	5e19	...
Ballater, ar.	5 0	5 51	6 45	...	5 0	1 30	Milltimber .	...	10 41	...	...
							Murtle .	...	10 50	...	...
							Cults .	...	11 0	...	...
							Holburn St.	...	...	...	...
							Aberdeen, ar.	9 38	11 20	5 32	3 15

e Passing time.
d Stops for Crossing purposes only.
e Collect Tickets from Passengers joining.
T Collect and examine Tickets.
† Stops where required to set down Passengers from south of Aberdeen on notice being given to the Guard.
* Stops to lift Passengers for south of Aberdeen on notice being given to the Stationmaster.

4·35 p.m. Passenger Train from Aberdeen to Banchory will be superseded by the above 4·35 p.m. Express.

On Sundays the Engine to work 3·30 a.m. and 12·20 p.m. Down Trains will come from Kittybrewster, and Engine of 2·0 p.m. Up Train will, on arrival at Aberdeen, run to Kittybrewster.

3·30 a.m. Down (Week-days and Sundays) Train is *not* to be signalled on the Block Telegraph and Train Tablet Instruments, but must get the proper fixed signals.

ON WEEK-DAYS, Stationmaster, Park, must telegraph the passing of 3·30 a.m. Down Train to Stationmaster, Aberdeen; and Stationmaster, Ballater, must telegraph its arrival to Stationmasters, Banchory and Park; and until the former advice has been received no Down Deeside Train must be allowed to leave Aberdeen, nor until receipt of the latter advice must a Down Train leave Park or an Up Train leave Banchory. ON SUNDAYS, Stationmaster, Ballater, must telegraph to Stationmaster, Aberdeen, the arrival of the 3·30 a.m. Down Train, and until this report has been received, no Down Deeside Train must be allowed to leave Aberdeen. No Up Train must be allowed to leave Ballater on Week-days and Sundays until 3·30 a.m. Down Train has arrived thereat. [Continued on page 2.

Supplement to the working timetable, 1912, showing the arrangements for the King's Messenger trains

The messengers—officially Queen's (or King's) special trains—had a life of seventy-two years, running from 1865 until 1937. In 1938 it was decided that the increased reliability of road transport made the provision of a special train unnecessary, and the old system of sending the courier over the hills by road was resumed.

Although latterly the messenger trains were not advertised in the public timetables, from the early days when a first-class coach was added, the company included them in its timetables and for many years they also appeared in Bradshaw. By the end of the nineteenth century, third-class accommodation was also being included.

In 1883, as a result of their being both publicly advertised and non-stop, the trains appeared as central points of debate in a remarkable lawsuit. Under the feu charter granted to the railway for the building of the public station at Crathes it had been stipulated that all trains should call at that station and, following correspondence between Sir Robert Burnett of Leys and the company in 1878, the subsidised services—primarily the messengers—had been advertised to call either regularly or conditionally at Crathes.

In 1882 the Great North provided a Saturdays only half-day excursion to Ballater, stopping only at Banchory and Aboyne. When the company refused Sir Robert's request that this train should stop at Crathes, he applied to the Court of Session in Edinburgh for an order requiring all trains except those privately chartered to call at Crathes unconditionally. The defence submitted by the Great North was that the schedules of the subsidised services were not entirely under its control and that the Saturday excursion had appeared in the timetables in error, being not available to ordinary fare-paying passengers.

The company won its case, but Lord Bramwell finally gave judgment in 1885 following an appeal to the House of Lords. He allowed the plea for the omission of the stop by the excursion service but reversed the previous finding in respect of the messengers. The terms of the feu charter were thereafter followed to the letter until 1914, when Sir Robert's successor to the estates, Sir Thomas Burnett, agreed to waive his rights and as a result some of the fast regular trains no longer stopped at Crathes.

EXCURSIONS ON DEESIDE

From the very first days when a railway was proposed to run along Deeside it was expected that holiday and tourist traffic would form a substantial part of the potential revenue of the line. The

Aberdeen Herald commented in 1850 that the line would 'afford to the inhabitants of Aberdeen an opportunity of breathing the fresh air in a climate milder than their own, and amidst some of the finest scenery in the world', and so it turned out.

Right from the outset the company made a bid for tourist traffic, and alongside the newspaper announcement of the opening on 8 September the *Aberdeen Herald* of 10 September 1853 carried notices of two such excursions. The railway itself organised 'ON TUESDAY, 13th curt., a TRAIN of FIRST-CLASS CARRIAGES' which ran to and from Banchory non-stop, leaving Ferryhill at 2.30 pm and returning at 8.30 pm, while the following day there was a 'PLEASURE TRIP to UPPER BANCHORY, under the auspices of the ABERDEEN TEMPERANCE SOCIETY'. This was open to 'Members of the above Society, and others friendly to its objects', and left Ferryhill at 11 am, and Banchory at 6.30 pm. Return fares were only three-quarters of the normal single fare. A week later, an announcement appeared regarding excursion trains for the 'Annual Gathering and Games' at Banchory, the return service being arranged to connect with the train south on the Aberdeen Railway. This began a long tradition of train services for the highland games on Deeside.

Another tradition began in the following July when it was announced that 'ON MONDAY, 17th JULY, EXCURSION TICKETS will be issued from ABERDEEN, by the 7.30, 11.0 A.M., and 4 P.M. Trains, to all the STATIONS on the Line, at which the Trains are advertised to stop'. This concession was for the Aberdeen Annual Holiday.

The following week's issue of the *Aberdeen Herald* (22 July) reported that

> Monday was observed in this city, especially by the shop-keeping interest, as a holiday . . . The day was devoted by most to railway excursions. We hear that . . . 56 carriages took 1,700 along the beautiful route of the Deeside line—for the most part to Banchory. The weather was very propitious for the excursionists. Banchory was never known to be so crowded with visitors.

Aberdeen holidays continued to provide heavy traffic for the line, and in Great North days trains would be made up on these occasions of almost any old stock that could be gathered together. It has been said that some of the original Deeside Railway coaches even survived until the first world war, being used for this service.

In the early years of this century, four sets of sixteen coaches were used to provide thirteen trains in the day, capable of carrying some 7,000 passengers to Banchory, together with the traffic to Ballater.

Writing in 1927 in *The Deeside Field*, Robert Gordon recollected seeing

> on two successive occasions of an Aberdeen holiday, trains of thirty-six and thirty-seven fully-loaded coaches, each drawn by two engines. On each of these occasions, a rider of the high spider bicycle, then coming into use, could have allowed a good handicap and finished the race a clear winner.

In 1860, when the line to Aboyne was opened, the company cashed in on its reputation as a Royal line with an excursion to see the Queen's arrival. In a notice headed 'Her Majesty's Journey to Balmoral' it was advertised that

> ON WEDNESDAY, 8th August, being the day on which Her Majesty will travel from Edinburgh to Balmoral, EXCURSION TICKETS will be issued from ABERDEEN to ABOYNE, by the Train leaving Aberdeen at 11.15 AM.

DEESIDE RAILWAY.

PLEASURE TRIP to UPPER BANCHORY, under the auspices of the ABERDEEN TEMPERANCE SOCIETY, on WEDNESDAY first, 14th curt. Fares to Banchory and back One Shilling, Third Class; One and Sixpence, First Class. The Train will leave Ferryhill Station, at Eleven, A.M., and Banchory at 6·30, P.M.

Members of the above Society, and others friendly to its objects, may obtain Tickets from Messrs. GEORGE MAITLAND, 40, Broad Street; JOHN M'DONALD, Confectioner, Market Buildings; JOHN M'QUARRIE, Clothier, Correction Wynd; WILLIAM LINDSAY, Bookseller, Gallowgate; GEORGE HENRY, Bookseller, Broad Street; and at the Deeside Railway Office.

W. B. FERGUSON, Manager.

Aberdeen 10:h Sept., 1853.

Newspaper announcement of the first rail excursion on Deeside, 1853

It was later reported that 'A special train had also brought out a number of people from Aberdeen, who, with those from the neighbourhood, formed a very considerable assemblage' when the royal party arrived at Aboyne.

The year 1854 also saw a magnanimous act on the part of the directors who granted the use of 'one third-class carriage . . . *gratis*' for 'an excursion to Banchory and back for the benefit of the Blind' attending the Aberdeen Asylum for the Blind.

At the turn of the century excursions were run to the Loch of

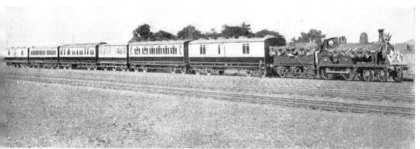

Page 91 : ROYAL SCENES

(30) *Arrival of the Czar and Czarina at Ballater,* 1896
(31) GNS *Royal train used for the opening of Marischal College,* 1906
(32) *King George VI inspecting the guard in Ballater station square,* 1938

Page 92 : ROYAL TRAINS

(33) *Down Royal train on Dinnet Muir, with west coast stock*
(34) *Last steam-hauled Royal train near Glassel, 1962*
(35) *The last Royal train on Deeside passing Ruthrieston station, 1965*

Aboyne, both in summer and winter. A platform existed at this time by the loch-side and in the summer was known as 'Loch of Aboyne Platform'. In the winter the loch was a popular centre for curling and special trains ran for the Bonspiels, the platform being known as the 'Curlers' Platform', and cheap fares also being allowed to skaters travelling there.

No note of the excursions on Deeside would be complete without reference to the combined rail-road round tours run by the Great North of Scotland Railway. The company had operated buses since 1904, when somewhat primitive motor buses were run between Ballater and Braemar each weekday in conjunction with the trains.

In June 1907 the company announced its 'Three Rivers Tour'. This was scheduled to operate 'By Rail, Motor, and Coach, *via* the Dee, Don and Spey, daily, from 1 July to 30 September'. The tour was a two-day affair which took in some of the finest scenery in the country. A motor bus left Ballater at 9.15 am to connect at Dinnet with the 8.5 am train from Aberdeen. Passengers then travelled on the bus *via* Strathdon to Cockbridge and then changed to a coach as the road gradients from thereon were too severe for the bus. Climbing to Tomintoul by way of the magnificent Lecht road, the coach arrived at this highest village in the highlands at 4.45 pm and passengers stayed the night there. The following day the tour continued by 'Motor Char-a-banc to Ballindalloch' and thence by rail to either Grantown-on-Spey or direct to Aberdeen. The route could be reversed if so desired and the fare for the round trip was 20s first-class, or 15s third-class.

A 'Deeside and Donside Day Circular Tour. By Rail and Motor' was also very popular. Inaugurated about 1910, this tour also ran *via* Dinnet and Strathdon, continued by motor to Alford and went on by rail from there to Aberdeen. Again the route could be reversed if desired, and for the eleven-hour day out the fare was 12s first-class and 9s third-class. Both of these rail and road combined tours were run from July to September only and were suspended after the 1914 season: they were never re-introduced.

After the 1914-18 war, excursion traffic—like many other aspects of the railway's operations—never recovered its pre-war eminence. The Aberdeen holidays continued to supply extra traffic, and private excursions (such as Sunday School outings) were run from time to time, but in the line's latter days British Railways made virtually no attempt to reclaim any of the tourist traffic that flooded into Deeside.

F

CHAPTER 5

Royal Trains

QUEEN VICTORIA

The Deeside line was always a 'Royal' line, sovereigns and other royalty travelling frequently along it to and from Balmoral Castle.

The first Royal journey on the line was undertaken only a month after the line opened for traffic by HRH The Duchess of Kent—Queen Victoria's mother—on Tuesday, 11 October 1853. Two days later, on Thursday 13, Queen Victoria and Prince Albert with 'the Royal family, and suite' travelled along the line.

Great preparations had been made for this auspicious occasion and the Queen was received by Mr Innes of Raemoir, Convenor of the County of Kincardine, and the chairman and directors of the railway company at Banchory.

> The station was beautifully decorated, and the scene was very animated, the weather being fine . . . The entrance through which the Royal party drove up was surmounted by a triumphal arch, with the crown in the centre, and other appropriate devices. The platform from where Her Majesty entered to the State carriage was laid with crimson cloth.

The train pulled out at 12.15 'amid loud cheers' and all along the line 'crowds of the lieges were assembled, and testified their loyalty in a hearty manner'. The train arrived at Ferryhill at 12.43, where a large collection of dignitaries awaited Her Majesty together with a guard of honour. After acknowledging the crowds, 'the engine having been attached, the signal was given, and the train moved off about three minutes after arrival'. This procedure remained much the same for many years, frequent reference being found to 'the hearty plaudits' of the spectators and also in the early years, to 'the Deeside engines, handsomely decorated with wreaths of evergreens and flowers'.

At Ferryhill, the Lord Provost, sheriffs and other dignitaries of the city were in attendance together with the guard of honour

Large crowds gathered outside the barriers—there being no permanent platform at this point after 1854—and 'It is needless to say that most loyal homage was done to Her Majesty by the spectators' (*Aberdeen Journal*, 15 August 1860). In the enclosure itself the privileged few with their ladies were permitted a closer look as Her Majesty usually 'graciously acknowledged' the greetings of the assembly.

On Wednesday, 8 August 1860, the Queen travelled north from Edinburgh and for the first time travelled through to Aboyne, the line having been opened in the previous December. The *Aberdeen Journal* reported that:

> The speed, as far as Banchory, was fast; but, on coming to the new Deeside Extension line, upon which Her Majesty had not previously travelled, the rate of movement was slackened, and a series of views of scenery, probably not equalled on any other railway, were very satisfactorily obtained.

The train reached Aboyne at 3.00 pm, 'being sharp time—after a very easy and pleasant journey,' where the Queen was greeted with customary enthusiasm. We are told that 'the new station—itself extensive and tasteful—was neatly decorated with heather'. The usual civic dignitaries, guard of honour and crowd—augmented by the travellers on a special excursion from Aberdeen for the occasion—greeted the Royal visitors who were served lunch 'in the station rooms (which included four suites, designed partly with a view to such an occasion)' before driving off for Balmoral.

The Queen and Prince Albert normally visited Balmoral every summer using the east coast route but after the Prince Consort died in 1861 her Majesty travelled north twice a year—spring and autumn—the first spring journey being made shortly after her bereavement, on 4 April 1862, by the west coast route which she always used thereafter. There were no greetings at Ferryhill and 'no demonstrations whatever' along the line, 'Her Majesty's wishes in this respect, being strictly observed by the people'.

The Queen continued to use Aboyne as the terminus of her rail journey even after the line was opened to Ballater, her first journey to the new terminus being on Friday, 23 August, 1867, almost a year after its opening, when she came to Deeside from a visit to the border counties. On 18 June, however, at the end of the visit made earlier that year, the Royal servants had travelled from Ballater to Aboyne by train, which Her Majesty then joined, having travelled thus far by coach. On 23 August the train arrived at 8 pm at Ballater where, after 'partaking of refreshments at the station' the Queen 'posted to Balmoral'. It is reported that 'A considerable number of the people of Ballater, at present crowded with visitors, turned out to welcome Her Majesty once more to Deeside, and give her a loyal cheer'. Thereafter Her Majesty continued to use Ballater as the terminus of her rail journey.

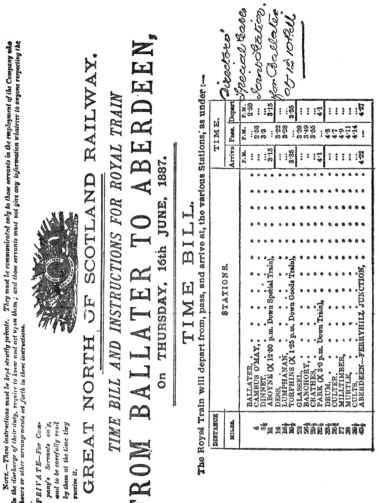

Time bill for the Royal train, 1887

Apart from our own Royal family, royalty of other countries also visited Deeside. The first of these visits began on Friday, 19 July 1889, when the 'King of Kings'. His Imperial Majesty the Shah of Persia, travelled from Ferryhill to Ballater. Travelling from Stirling, the King's train was expected at Ferryhill at 4 pm and, long before that time, a huge crowd was gathered. The Lord Provost and town council were present

and, as soon as the train drew up a small platform, railed and covered with crimson cloth, was raised to the height of the carriage floor,

and the civic dignitaries ascended and greeted His Majesty. An address of welcome inscribed on calfskin was read and presented to the Shah, who must have made a striking figure,

dressed in a dark military uniform . . . over which he wore a flowing military cloak sufficiently open to display the large emeralds worn on his breast. In his Astrakhan cap the Shah wore a large Persian crest richly encrusted with diamonds.

After conversing through his interpreter with the Lord Provost, the Shah entered his train, which moved off 'amid the heavy cheers of the assemblage and the strains of the pibroch'. At Ballater, His Majesty was greeted by Prince Albert Victor of Wales and Mr McKenzie, both in highland dress, and a large crowd of local citizens.

The Shah returned along the line on Monday, 22 July, which was the Aberdeen local holiday. The Royal party reached Ballater at 11.45 am, which was 'much earlier than was expected . . . Indeed, so unexpectedly soon did the visitors reach Ballater, that the guard of honour . . . had not yet arrived from the barracks'.

The party entered the special train, which was waiting, and, on the arrival of the guard of honour, the Shah went out and inspected it. The train was due to arrive at Ferryhill at 1.58, but 'probably owing to the heavy holiday traffic' (over 7,000 tourists visited Deeside that day), it was slightly delayed, 'and she drew up at the usual place eleven minutes late'. The Lord Provost presented His Majesty with a basket of strawberries while the engines were being changed and, to the plaudits of the crowd, 'the train moved slowly off after a stay of four minutes'.

The next—and most notable—visit of foreign Royalty was in 1896 when the Czar of Russia visited Queen Victoria at Balmoral. Nicolas II, Czar of all the Russias, was married to Princess Alix of Hesse, Queen Victoria's granddaughter and, although the beautiful Czarina was welcomed 'home', the Czar himself was very far from welcome. As the press noted, 'The Tsar is a political personage whose unlimited power exceeds that of any other monarch on earth'. Furthermore at that time, as a result of events in Turkey, Russia was held in odium in this country.

The arrangements made at Ballater were very extensive. The station was decorated in yellow and black (the Imperial colours) and a covered porch had been added at the entrance from the square. Indeed it was said that: 'Those who are familiar with Ballater Station in its normal state would, if they saw it now, hardly recognise it'. The final touch was the installation of electric lighting for the occasion, with the square lit as well as the station, together with the road as far as the burgh boundary. The power came from a generator which received steam from a Great North engine in the station.

Because of the risk of trouble from the Nihilists, very strict safety precautions were taken. Linesmen were posted all along the track and the stations were cleared of everyone not on essential business. At Ferryhill only a very limited number of dignitaries was present, and at Ballater the crowds were kept well back from the station itself. The Czar landed at Leith, where he was met by the Prince of Wales, and his train reached Ferryhill at 5.34 pm. 22 September 1896 was a notable day in that its end marked Queen Victoria becoming the longest reigning British sovereign (having been on the throne since 20 June 1837), but the weather was anything but Royal, there being drenching rain all day. As *Bon Accord* put it, 'even the heavens wept'.

In view of the inclement weather a roof was hastily added to the temporary platform at Ferryhill during the day. As the train came into view it was seen that in front of the leading locomotive was mounted a placard with the words 'Royal Train' and miniature Russian and British standards fluttered from the sides. The royal visitors did not leave the train but the Czar—wearing the uniform of a colonel of the Scots Greys—came forward to receive the address of welcome. The Prince of Wales was in the uniform of the 25th Dragoons of Kieff, of which he was Colonel-in-Chief.

At Cults and West Cults stations 'a good number of people had assembled' but beyond there, darkness intervened and there were no more demonstrations before Ballater. The guard of honour —a hundred men of the Black Watch—was drawn up 'promptly at seven o'clock'. After being received by the Duke and Duchess of York the royal party entered its carriages and went in torch-light procession to Balmoral.

For the return journey on 3 October there was much less fuss. The train, 'consisting of 15 finely-appointed saloons and a number of composites and luggage vans' was drawn up ready. The Czar and Czarina arrived about 11 pm and, after some presentations were made, the train steamed off as 'the band of the Black Watch again sent forth the strains of the Russian National Hymn'. At Aberdeen there was no ceremonial at all. The train pulled into the joint station at 12.22 and, after a quick inspection, moved off at 12.29. The local police must have heaved very hearty sighs of relief at seeing Their Imperial Majesties off their territory without incident.

Queen Victoria made her last journey along Deeside on Tuesday, 7 November 1900, on her way to Windsor. Her Majesty—who was dressed in deep mourning—had expressed a desire to leave privately, with no one on the platform, and when the train left at 3.30 it was with the minimum of fuss. At Ferryhill Junction there was a light drizzle and a 'large gathering' of spectators. The Queen did not leave the train when it pulled in at 4.47 'drawn by two powerful locomotives' and, after a stay of five minutes, 'the train moved away without any demonstrations on the part of the spectators'. Her Majesty went from Windsor to Osborne on the Isle of Wight and died a little more than two months after saying farewell to the highland home which she had loved and visited annually for over fifty years.

KING EDWARD VII

King Edward VII went to Balmoral only once a year, in the autumn. His first visit was made in September 1901. The train from London arrived at the joint station at 9.15 am on the 28th and the King breakfasted in the Palace Hotel, while Queen Alexandra remained in the saloon for her meal. Punctually at 10 am, the train left for Deeside with little ceremony. Thereafter during the King's reign Ferryhill continued to be the exchange point as hitherto.

Although the day began wet, by the time Ballater was reached at eleven o'clock the sun had come out, a large crowd had gathered 'and Kodaks were largely in evidence'. A floral arch had been erected and was adorned with stags' heads. The King was in highland dress and, after inspecting the guard of honour, he escorted the Queen to their carriage and 'loud cheers renewed again and again were raised as the Royal party drove off'.

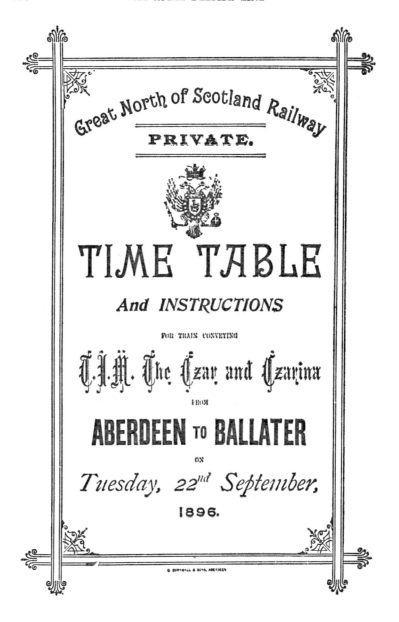

Great North of Scotland Railway

PRIVATE.

TIME TABLE

And INSTRUCTIONS

FOR TRAIN CONVEYING

T.I.M. The Czar and Czarina

FROM

ABERDEEN TO BALLATER

ON

Tuesday, 22nd September,

1896.

G. CORNWALL & SONS, ABERDEEN

Pages from the working tim

Great North of Scotland Railway.

For Company's Servants only, and to be carefully read by them at the time they receive it.

NOTE.—*These instructions must be kept strictly private. They must be communicated only to those Servants in the employment of the Company who in the discharge of their duty require to know and act upon them; and those Servants must not give any information whatever to anyone respecting the hours or other arrangements set forth in these instructions.*

TIME BILL AND INSTRUCTIONS

FOR TRAIN CONVEYING

T.I.M. THE CZAR AND CZARINA OF RUSSIA,

From Aberdeen to Ballater,

ON TUESDAY, 22nd SEPTEMBER, 1896.

The IMPERIAL TRAIN will depart from, pass, and arrive at the various Stations, as under:—

Distance. MILES.	STATIONS.	TIME Arrive.	TIME Pass.	TIME Depart.
		P.M.	P.M.	P.M.
	ABERDEEN—FERRYHILL JUNCTION,	5 31	..	5 50
¾	HOLBURN STREET,	...	5 52	...
3	CULTS,	...	5 55	...
4¾	MURTLE,	...	5 57	...
5¾	MILLTIMBER,	..	5 58	...
6⅞	CULTER,	...	6 0	..
9¼	DRUM,	...	6 4	...
10¼	PARK,	...	6 6	..
13¾	CRATHES,	...	6 11	...
16¼	BANCHORY (Cross 6·15 p.m. Up Banchory Train at Banchory),	6 16	...	6 16
20¾	GLASSEL,	...	6 24	...
23¼	TORPHINS (Pass 3·13 p.m. Down Goods Train at Torphins),	...	6 27	...
26¼	LUMPHANAN (Cross 5·25 p.m. (5·50 p.m. altered) Up Train at Lumphanan),	6 35	...	6 33
28⅞	DESS,	...	6 36	...
31¾	ABOYNE,	...	6 41	...
36¼	DINNET,	...	6 49	...
38¾	CAMBUS O'MAY,	...	6 52	...
42⅝	BALLATER,	7 0	...	...

NOTES OF WORKING.

IMPERIAL TRAIN.—The time of passing Intermediate Stations and of arrival at Ballater must be strictly observed.

The Engine Whistle is not to be sounded on approaching Signals or otherwise, except in emergency.

DOWN TRAIN.—The 3·13 p.m. Down Goods Train must be shunted into the Siding at Torphins until the Imperial Train, due at 6·27 p.m., has passed Torphins.

UP TRAINS.—The 6·15 p.m. Up Train is to remain at Banchory to cross the Imperial Train, due at 6·16 p.m.

The 5·25 p.m. (5·50 p.m. altered) Up Train is to stop at Lumphanan to cross the Imperial Train, due at 6·33 p.m.

The Engines for Imperial Train are to leave the Joint Station for Ferryhill Junction at 4·55 p.m.

Czar of Russia's visit, 1896

During the reign of King Edward VII the Great North of Scotland Railway itself provided Royal trains on at least ten occasions—a particular honour for such a small company. The first such train was on the occasion of the King's first journey north after his coronation. Because of His Majesty's serious illness the coronation had been postponed at the last moment and, after it finally took place on 9 August 1902, the King and Queen cruised round the west coast on the Royal yacht, *en route* for their home at Balmoral. When they landed at Invergordon Their Majesties boarded a train supplied by the Great North.

As the King had asked for the visit to be private there was little ceremony but, at Aberdeen, the Lord Provost and magistrates 'deemed it expedient to attend, as on former occasions when the reigning monarch was passing, in order to pay their respects to the King and Queen'. After a pause of ten minutes the train pulled out at 3.30 pm. At Ballater there was even less formality, although a large crowd assembled to view the Royal arrival at 4.30 (report in *Aberdeen Journal*, 15 September 1902).

During that autumn's visit Royal trains were supplied for Queen Alexandra and the Prince of Wales for private visits made by them to Dalmeny and Fochabers respectively.

The company's proudest moment came in 1903 when it received a request from the General Manager of the Great Northern Railway 'applying for the use of the company's royal train'. The King was staying at Rufford Abbey in Derbyshire and attending Doncaster races before his journey north. The GNS naturally made the maximum use of this request in its publicity, even claiming that the 'King commanded the use of the Royal train'.

The train travelled south and collected His Majesty at King's Cross on 7 September 1903, travelling then to Ollerton in Derbyshire, and thence daily to Doncaster and back for the next three days. On the 14th the train travelled back north, arriving at Aberdeen at 4.55 pm.

> It was arranged that no stoppage should on this occasion take place at Ferryhill Junction, as had been the case when the late Queen Victoria travelled to Deeside, but that the train should come into the Joint Station—an arrangement that proved perfectly convenient to all concerned.

Again the city magistrates were officially represented on the occasion.

> A minute or two before the scheduled time the Royal train steamed slowly into the station, and the fine saloon in which His

Majesty travelled, belonging to the Great North of Scotland Railway Company, at once arrested the eye by its handsome proportions and chaste appointments.

After a brief pause for the engines to be changed the train left again for Ballater where a large crowd waited 'which included contingents from all the stations from Banchory onwards and from the districts beyond Ballater'. The crowd was indeed the largest to greet Royal visitors at Ballater for many years.

On September 27 1906, the last Royal train put on by the Great North for a reigning sovereign ran from Ballater to Aberdeen and back, the occasion being the opening of the new buildings of Marischal College on the occasion of its quarter-centenary. The history of Scottish Universities is of more than respectable antiquity, it being truly said that Aberdeen had two universities at a time when the whole of England had no more.

The train provided for the occasion was similar to that used in 1903, and the single locomotive hauling it was heavily decorated with evergreens, a crown in front of the chimney, and the royal coat of arms and crossed flags mounted above the front buffer beam. Although it left Ballater six minutes late it arrived at Holburn Street at 12.15, exactly on time, 'and was drawn up opposite the covered way'. The *Aberdeen Free Press* reported the next day that

> the valley of the Dee was bathed in sunshine yesterday morning. The most distant points in a district which Royalty has made famous and historic were clearly outlined on one of the most beautiful of autumn days.

This was the first occasion on which a Royal train used Holburn Street station, and it was lavishly decorated for the occasion. After the procession through the decorated streets and the ceremony at Marischal College, the royal visitors lunched at the Town House and processed to the joint station for the return journey. Here again elaborate decorations had been erected, and the King had presented to him 'a number of distinguished French guests who, during last week, were in Aberdeen attending the meetings of the Franco-Scottish Society'. The train eventually 'glided out of the station' at 3.41 pm and arrived at Ballater at 4.45, where there was 'a large gathering of people' waiting to watch Their Majesties arrive.

All the Royal trains provided by the Great North thereafter were for Queen Alexandra and the Prince of Wales. Each year, from 1907 to 1910, the Queen travelled from Ballater to Dundee, whence she sailed on the royal yacht for Copenhagen. Although her father, King Christian IX of Denmark, had died in 1906, Queen Alexandra had purchased a house near Copenhagen where every autumn she met her sister, the Dowager Empress of Russia.

King Edward VII made his last journey on the Deeside line on 11 October 1909, when returning to London by day. More Royal trains had been run on Deeside during the nine years of his reign than in any other comparable period of the line's history and during this period the timing between Aberdeen and Ballater for Royal trains reached its fastest, at around 1 hour 5 min.

The last Great North Royal train ran on 19 September 1910, for Queen Alexandra, then the Queen Mother.

KING GEORGE V

King George V made his first visit to Deeside as King only three months after his accession, arriving at Ferryhill at 8.30 am on Tuesday 9 August 1910 in the largest Royal train that had ever passed through Aberdeen. It comprised twelve saloons and measured 808 ft 8 in overall—equal to the length of an ordinary train of twenty vehicles. The *Aberdeen Free Press* reported that 'At Ferryhill one of the two splendid engines substituted by the Great North of Scotland Railway Company was No 31, newly turned out of the workshops at Inverurie. The Royal train was the first which it had drawn'.

The day was exceptionally fine and a very large crowd was gathered at Ballater. The King and Queen were met by the Marquis of Huntly and, while His Majesty inspected the Guard of Honour, a group of 300 schoolchildren sang the National Anthem 'very sweetly'. The King, Queen Mary and the remainder of the party then entered their carriage and 'drove away to Balmoral, amid ringing cheers'.

During 1913 the Dowager Empress of Russia accompanied Queen Alexandra the Queen Mother (her sister) on a visit to Balmoral, travelling from Wolferton.

The year 1913 also marked the last visit of the King to Deeside for several years. Although he visited Scapa Flow, Rosyth and Clydeside during the war His Majesty did not come to his holiday home on Deeside again until August 1919. After the years of war and the busy months that followed the King and Queen were to have a purely private and quiet holiday at Balmoral, and the district was overjoyed to have the Royal visitors on Deeside again. The train from Euston arrived at Ferryhill Junction at 9.10 am on Tuesday, 19 August. It was the heaviest Royal train then to have travelled along Deeside, consisting of twelve coaches and weighing about 500 tons. During the ten minutes' stay at Ferryhill two Great North engines, decorated with flags and bearing the Royal arms, were attached in place of the Caledonian engines, and the King (wearing Highland dress) and Queen Mary conversed with the Lord Provost and other dignitaries.

At Ballater, the station and its vicinity were thronged with crowds waiting in the beautiful weather. The *Aberdeen Free Press* commented that 'the Royal party had an opportunity of seeing Deeside at its best'. The station had been lavishly decorated with 'tasteful drapings of Royal Stuart tartan and an ornamental shield bearing the letters in gold, GR, and a crown in gold cloth'. His Majesty's feelings on viewing the drapings as he stepped from the saloon wearing his kilt, also of Stuart tartan, are not recorded. The train was a quarter of an hour late, arriving at 10.45, and it was explained that the late arrival was due to the train's weight. The King and Queen were enthusiastically received and were obviously in excellent humour. After inspecting the guard (and chatting with Corporal Ritchie of the Seaforth Highlanders, who had won the VC on the Somme), the Royal party drove by motor car to Balmoral.

The weight of Royal trains had more or less doubled since the end of Queen Victoria's reign and as a result of this the scheduled time for the journey was increased until it took longer than even the old Queen's had done. In 1920 the practice of exchanging engines at Ferryhill was at last abandoned and thereafter the exchange was made in the joint station.

In 1929 the King and Queen came to Aberdeen to open the museum extension to the art gallery, and Cowdray Hall. On 29 September, Their Majesties' special train arrived at Holburn Street —again lavishly decorated—at 3.25 pm and was welcomed by a guard of honour, the Lord Provost and magistrates of the city. As on the occasion of King Edward VII's visit to open the Marischal College buildings twenty-three years earlier, the return journey was made from the joint station.

King George V travelled along the Deeside line for the last time on Friday 27 September 1935. Their Majesties departed from Ballater to the sound of cheers and at Aberdeen also 'rousing cheers were given as the Royal train drew out of the station'.

KING EDWARD VIII

The seventy-year-old King George died on 20 January 1936 and was succeeded by the Prince of Wales as King Edward VIII. Although he reigned for less than a year the new King visited Deeside in the autumn, as had three generations of his predecessors. When the Royal train arrived at Aberdeen at 7.10 am on Saturday 19 September there was a huge crowd waiting to greet its new sovereign. The *Evening Express* that day reported that

> Sincere and wholehearted as always is the welcome which an Aberdeen station gathering gives its Sovereign when he comes north for his annual holiday on Deeside, this morning's was undoubtedly the greatest of them all.

The King, who was accompanied by his brother the Duke of York (the future King George VI, who was to open Aberdeen's new Royal Infirmary at Foresterhill on the following Wednesday) was so pleased with the welcome that he and the Duke stepped out on to the platform to salute the crowd. After a stop of ten minutes the train moved off for Ballater, again to renewed cheering. At Ballater station 'from practically the whole population of Ballater a cheer arose which almost drowned the bagpipe music accompanying the Royal Salute given by the guard of honour'. Both King and Duke were wearing kilts and plaids of Balmoral tartan and they drove off by car to Balmoral.

The following Monday the Duke and Duchess of Kent passed through Aberdeen for Balmoral, again to a warm welcome from a large crowd at Aberdeen (comprised mainly of women) and 'rousing cheers' at Ballater. The couple travelled in a reserved carriage in the ordinary Deeside train leaving at 8.10 am.

This Royal holiday was only a short one, for on Wednesday, 1 October the King, accompanied by the Duke and Duchess of Kent, 'was given an enthusiastic send off', the train leaving Ballater at 6.20 pm and arriving at Aberdeen at 7.35. Again an enthusiastic crowd greeted His Majesty. Here the eight carriages that comprised the special train were attached to the front of the ordinary LMS 7.47 pm train for Euston. Speaking to a police inspector at Perth later the King said, 'I have been up only a fortnight, but it was quite enjoyable. I am not tied down and I can travel to Scotland any time I like. I intend to make more frequent visits to Scotland in the future'. Alas, it was not to be. On 10 December 1936 he signed an instrument of abdication and was succeeded by his brother, the Duke of York.

KING GEORGE VI

The new King, George VI (the third monarch to reign during the year 1936), made his first visit along Deeside after his accession by road from Aberdeen Joint Station on Wednesday 4 August 1937. The visit was a long one for it was Monday, 11 October before the return journey, which was made by train. At Ballater station a number of presentations were made, while at Aberdeen a large crowd waited at the joint station and the train pulled out to loud cheers. The following year (1938), the Royal party arrived in Aberdeen by sea—the first time a reigning sovereign had done so for ninety years—and again made the journey to Balmoral by road. This year the King broke his holiday to return south for the funeral of Prince Arthur of Connaught, making the journey by rail on Thursday 15 September, the same day that Neville Chamberlain flew to Germany to see Herr Hitler about the latter's claims for the Sudetenland—having travelled south in a special saloon attached to the ordinary night train.

In 1939 the King came to Deeside by train for the first time since his accession. The Royal train arrived at Aberdeen Joint Station at 7.30 am on Tuesday 1 August and, although the platform was crowded, the civic representatives were not present and the Royal family was not seen during the ten minutes taken for the engines to be changed. At Drum the train stopped for about an hour for breakfast to be served, and the seventy or so people who had gathered there were delighted when Princess Elizabeth and Princess Margaret left the train accompanied by a governess and played on the platform, where they were later joined by the King and Queen. The Aberdeen *Evening Express* that day reported that 'Ballater made up for the welcome Aberdeen had been unable to give'. A large crowd assembled in the sunshine watched as the King, in Highland dress, inspected the Guard of Honour of the Royal Scots Fusiliers, and then the Royal family, accompanied by Princess Elizabeth's corgi, motored off for Balmoral. The holiday was to be only a short one, for the Queen and the Princesses left on the twelfth for Glamis and were joined there by the King on the fourteenth, after the opening of the grouse season. Less than three weeks later, on 3 September, the country was again at war.

August 1945 was a momentous time for the whole world. On the seventh and ninth of that month the first atomic bombs were exploded over Hiroshima and Nagasaki, and on the tenth the papers carried the headlines 'End of World War'. 'Capitulation in Japan'. It was amid feelings of widespread relief at the end of six years of war that the Royal family was welcomed to Deeside a fortnight later, on the twenty-fifth.

After a twenty-minute wait at Aberdeen, during which time Their Majesties were not seen, the train went on to Drum, where a halt was made for breakfast. At Ballater a guard of honour of young soldiers wearing the tartan flashes of all the Highland regiments on their battledress was drawn up and 'a large crowd filled the Station Square, which was bathed in sunshine'. The *Evening Express* reported that

> Deeside was looking its best. Bright sunshine painted a glorious picture in rich colours, the purple of the heather just reaching full bloom, the gold of ripe cornfields, and here and there a touch of autumn yellow among the varied greens of the woodland foliage.

After inspecting the Guard of Honour—the first ceremonial to be seen at Ballater since before the war—the Royal visitors were greeted by loud cheers as they drove off for Balmoral.

In the coming years the King and Queen spent several short holidays at Balmoral in May and early June—as had Queen Victoria after Prince Albert's death—as well as the traditional autumn visit.

The King's last visit to Deeside was in 1951, commencing on Friday, 3 August. When the train arrived at Ballater a crowd of about 2,000 greeted the King and Queen with cheers, as cameras recorded the scene for the Technicolor film 'Royal Scotland'. His Majesty looked fit after his recent long illness, but appeared thinner than when he had last visited Deeside.

During the holiday Princess Margaret celebrated her coming of age at Balmoral on 21 August, but the King's lung condition continued to trouble him. On 7 September he made an all-night train journey from Ballater to see his radiologist in London, and arrangements were made for him to travel south again by train for treatment on 14 September. In the event, a last-minute decision was made that he should fly from Aberdeen airport on the 15th, and he was joined in London by the Queen, who also travelled by air, four days later. The King's condition continued to give rise to alarm but by Christmas he appeared to be recovering well, and it came as a grievous shock to the nation when he died of a coronary

Page 109 : DIESEL AND ELECTRIC TRACTION

(36) *Battery electric railcar at Dinnet*
(37) *North British type 2 on freight train at Cults*
(38) *Diesel multiple-units at Glassel on the last day of passenger services*

Page 110: THE END

(39) *Stationmaster ringing the century-old handbell at Ballater for the last train*
(40) *The last passenger train leaving Ballater*
(41) *The last freight train entering Culter goods yard*

thrombosis in the early hours of 6 February 1952 at Sandringham.

QUEEN ELIZABETH

The new Queen, Elizabeth I of Scotland and Elizabeth II of England, made her first visit to Deeside, after succeeding to the throne, on Friday, 8 August 1952. The Royal train arrived at Aberdeen joint station at 7.55 and Prince Charles and Princess Anne waved and threw kisses to the crowd from the window while the engines were changed. The Duchess of Kent, with the Duke, Princess Alexandra and Prince Michael, were also at the station having travelled north in a special coach attached to the 'Aberdonian' night sleeper, which was attached to the ordinary Ballater train for the rest of the journey.

The Royal train itself arrived at Ballater in drenching rain, despite which a crowd of fully 1,200 had congregated to meet it. The guard of honour, of the Black Watch, was inspected by the Duke of Edinburgh, and the Queen's car left for Balmoral to a fresh burst of cheering. The Royal train left Ballater again to take Her Majesty to Doncaster for the St Leger on Friday, 12 September; that day also the Duke of Kent and his sister ended their Deeside holiday and left Ballater in a special coach attached to the 3.30 pm train. The following year, after the coronation, the Queen's arrival took place in beautiful weather on 5 August, and a crowd of over 2,000 greeted her at Ballater. Rumours had been rife that Her Majesty intended to sell Balmoral Castle, but she told the Marquis of Aberdeen that she had 'no intention of giving up her Scottish home on Deeside'. In the bright summer sunshine the Queen herself inspected the guard (of the Argyll & Sutherland Highlanders) before motoring to Balmoral.

Like her father, Queen Elizabeth did not always come to Balmoral by rail but frequently motored, and so it was that the last time the Royal train was steam-hauled on Deeside the Royal family was not on board. During their 1962 holiday the Queen and Prince Philip had returned to London for a few days and, on their return on 15 September, they left the train at Perth and the Duke drove Her Majesty to Balmoral, over the Devil's Elbow. The train came on to Ballater with the staff and was hauled along Deeside by two class 'B1' locomotives (Nos 61346 and 61400). Strictly this was not a Royal train but an express passenger train, and as such carried the ordinary class 'A' headlamp code.

The last Royal train on Deeside left Ballater at 7.15 pm on 15

G

October 1965. The Queen had arrived in Aberdeen two months previously on the Royal yacht *Britannia* and had motored to Balmoral. For the last Deeside Royal train, even the weather was in mourning. Hauled by two gleaming North British type 2 diesel locomotives (Nos D6142 and D6145), the train had arrived at Ballater during the afternoon, and a crowd of only some two hundred was gathered in the station square in a steady downpour of rain when the Queen drove up for her last rail journey along Deeside, in the dark. On the flower-decked platform, she chatted with the officials of the Royal burgh and of the railway, and 'after a brief farewell the Queen boarded the Royal train, but returned to an open window to wave goodbye' (*Press & Journal*, 16 October). Along the Dee valley the four headlamps that indicated a Royal train flashed past for the last time.

During 113 years six reigning sovereigns had used the Deeside railway to travel to and from their Highland home. Only the closing of the line itself brought an end to this chapter of the history of Royal Deeside.

CHAPTER 6

Closures

Apart from the closure of Ferryhill Junction and Mills of Drum in the formative years of the line (both as a result of the opening of stations elsewhere) it was 1937—nearly eighty-four years after the line opened—before there was any large-scale withdrawal of facilities on the Deeside line, and after that fourteen more years elapsed before the next closure. The 1960s however saw a rapidly-escalating series of withdrawals of freight and passenger services that culminated in the final closure of the line at the end of 1966.

The suburban services originally introduced in 1894 were the first to go, the final trains of this service running on Saturday, 3 April 1937. Increasing competition from buses had made the 'sub-bies' no longer a viable commercial proposition. Notice was given that sixteen down and seventeen up trains, between Aberdeen and Culter, plus an extra one in each direction on Saturdays only, would 'cease to run on and from Monday, 5 April, 1937', and that as a result of these withdrawals 'Holburn Street, Ruthrieston Halt, Pitfodels Halt, West Cults, Bieldside, Murtle Halt and Milltimber Stations will be closed'.

Although no ceremony had been planned the actual last trains aroused 'even less interest than had been expected', according to the *Press & Journal* the following Monday. The event was over-shadowed by the arrival at 10.45 pm—only five minutes before the last departure—of an excursion train carrying between 400 and 500 supporters of Aberdeen football club, who had just seen their team win a notable cup-tie victory at Edinburgh.

> The excursionists were met by a large crowd of friends, all eager to get first-hand news of the match, while all was bustle and excitement at that part of the station, platforms Nos 8 and 9, from which the Dyce and Culter trains left, were almost completely deserted up till a few minutes before the time of departure.

About sixty people travelled on the Culter train, and only half a dozen people were left on the two platforms after the trains had pulled out. At 10.50 there was 'a banging of doors, a shrill whistle' and the two trains steamed away simultaneously. The occasion was summed up by the *Press & Journal*'s sub-headings on the Monday. 'Little interest in event. Crowds engrossed in sport'. Thus ended nearly forty-three years of a remarkable service.

Following nationalisation, the first closure was the little-used station at Drum, in 1951. It was nearly nine years later, in July 1960, that freight services were withdrawn from Dess, but in 1964 the withdrawals began in earnest. British Railways had made no attempt to develop freight services; indeed it had apparently made efforts to lose the existing traffic either by refusing to handle or by putting a prohibitive price on much of the essential freight for the area (such as farm livestock). It came as no surprise in 1964 when freight services were withdrawn from Cults, Park, Crathes, Glassel, Lumphanan and Dinnet, as from 15 June, and, nine months later in March 1965, from Torphins. Freight services could be withdrawn with minimal notice and without reference to any outside body. The passenger services were another matter.

THE BEECHING REPORT AND ITS CONSEQUENCES

As part of the reorganisation of the British Transport Commission structure in 1961 the government appointed Dr Richard Beeching to be Chairman of the British Transport Commission. An investigation into the finances of the railways was made and, in 1963, Her Majesty's Stationery Office published the BRB's report on 'The Reshaping of British Railways'—the famous Beeching Report. This report listed a large number of lines and stations from which it was proposed that passenger services should be withdrawn. Among them was the Aberdeen-Ballater line.

On Deeside the report was received with dismay and, on 13 May 1963 a meeting was held at Aboyne between representatives of local authorities and other interested bodies. Strong opinions were expressed, both that withdrawal of services would cause considerable hardship and financial loss to the area, and that the present management of the line left a great deal to be desired. The meeting then appointed a committee to 'go into matters in greater detail and build up a case for the retention of the line' (minutes of the meeting). This joint committee—later to be called the Deeside Railway Preservation Committee—agreed that a survey should be

ABERDEEN TO BALLATER — WEEKDAYS — E95

E95

HEADCODE		2 B		2 B	2 B		2 B		2 B		2 B		2 B
		Battery Car		Diesel	Battery Car		Battery Car		Diesel		Battery Car	Runs DAILY 14th June to 7th October and P&O from 8th October	Diesel

Mileage M	C						SX		SO					
0	0	**ABERDEEN** .. .. .. dep	1	am 8 9		am 9 38	PM 1 55		PM 1 55		PM 3 45		PM 6 10	PM 8 35
0	51	Ferryhill Jn.	2	8 11	..	9 40	1 57	..	1 57	..	3 47	6 12	8 37
3	52	Cults	3	8 17		9 46					3 53	6 18	
7	38	Culter	4	8g127		9 53	2 5	..	2 5	..	4 0	6 25	8 47
10	62	Park	5	8 34		10 0	2 15		2 15		4 7	6X32	9VX35
13	76	Crathes	6	8 39		10 5					4 12		
16	72	Banchory	7	8 48		10 11	2 25		2 25		4gX22	6 43	9 10
17	30	Dee Street Halt	8	8 47		10 13	2 27		2 27		4 34	6 44	9 12
21	31	Glassel	9	8 56		10 22	2X36		2 36		4 33	6 53	9X20
23	66	Torphins	10	9 1		10 27	2 41		2 41		4 38	6 58	9 25
26	71	Lumphanan	11	9 8		10X34	2 48		2 48		4 45	7 5	9 33
29	47	Dess	12	9 12		10 38			2 52		4 49	7 9	
32	26	Aboyne	13	9 17		10 43	2 56		2 57		4 54	7 14	9 40
36	66	Dinnet	14	9 28		10 51	3 4		3 5		5 2	7 22	9 48
39	38	Cambus O' May Halt	15	9X31		10X57						7R28	
43	27	**BALLATER** .. .. arr	16	9 37		11 3	3 14		3 15		5 12	7 34	9 58

V—Arrive 8.54 pm. Call Not Advertised.

BALLATER TO ABERDEEN — WEEKDAYS

HEADCODE		2 B		2 B	2 B		2 B		2 B		2 B
		Diesel		Battery Car	Diesel		Battery Car		Diesel	Runs DAILY 14th June to 7th October and P&O from 8th October	Battery Car

Mileage M	C											
0	0	**BALLATER** .. .. .. dep	1	am 7 28		am 10 3	PM 12 30		PM 3 25		PM 5 33	PM 8 3
3	69	Cambus O' May Halt	2	7R27		10R10	12R37		3R32			
6	41	Dinnet	3	7 31		10 14	12 41		3 36		5 43	8 13
11	1	Aboyne	4	7 38		10 21	12 48		3 43		5 50	8 20
13	60	Dess	5	7 43		10 26	12 53		3 48			
16	36	Lumphanan	6	7 48		10AX36	12 58		3 53		6 0	8 30
19	41	Torphins	7	7 55		10 43	1 5		4 0		6 7	8 37
21	76	Glassel	8	8 0		10 48	1R10		4 5		6 12	
25	77	Dee Street Halt	9	8 7		10 55	1 17		4 12		6 19	8 47
26	35	Banchory	10	8 9		10 57	1 19		4X20		6 21	8 49
29	31	Crathes	11	8 14		11 2			4 25			
32	45	Park	12	8 19		11 7	1 28		4 30		6gX33	8X57
35	69	Culter	13	8X25		11 13	1 34		4 36		6 39	9 3
39	55	Cults	14	8 31		11 19			4 42			
42	56	Ferryhill Jn.	15	8 36		11 24	1 43		4 47		6 49	9 13
43	27	**ABERDEEN** .. .. arr	16	8 39		11 27	1 46		4 50		6 51	9 15

A—Arrives 10.30 am.
N—Arrives 4.14 pm.

Page from the last Deeside working timetable, 1965. (Note the reference to the battery railcar, withdrawn from the line three years previously) carried out by a management consultant on the running of the line, so that the case for retention might be built on factual grounds.

At the meeting of the committee on 2 December it was reported that the British Railways Board had officially intimated that it proposed to discontinue all railway passenger train services between Aberdeen and Ballater on and from 2 March 1964,

> and that any user of the rail service and any body representing such users desirous of objecting to the proposal might lodge an objection not later than 17 January 1964 with the Secretary of the Transport Users' Consultative Committee for Scotland.

Certain objections had already been lodged, with the result that the discontinuance of the rail service was deferred until after a hearing by the Transport Users' Consultative Committee and its report to the Minister of Transport.

On 21 January 1964 there was produced an interim report to the Deeside Railway Preservation Committee, followed by the full report on 29 March. Few documents so damning of railway mismanagement and extravagance can have been produced in recent years.

The main feelings of the people on Deeside were summed up thus '. . . the Deeside community quite justly feel that they should not be penalised on account of the failure of British Railways in the past to introduce effective cost reduction measures'.

At the TUCC hearing on 23 September 1964 all the evidence was produced. Unfortunately, the procedure at TUCC hearings is weighted heavily against the objectors, and only evidence as to hardship is admissible. Nevertheless, the committee was evenly divided, with four members in favour of closure and four against.

On 31 August 1965 the blow fell with a letter from the Ministry of Transport to British Railways Board. In this it was stated that the Minister (then Mr Tom Fraser)

> accepts the view of half the members of the Committee that having regard to the bus services at present being provided no appreciable hardship would arise from the closure if certain additional bus services were provided. He has therefore decided to give his consent to the closure subject to the conditions mentioned below.

The conditions were the provision of certain additional bus services.

This decision aroused widespread dismay and indignation on Deeside and a protracted but unavailing correspondence was taken

British Railways Board

PUBLIC NOTICE

Transport Act, 1962

WITHDRAWAL OF
RAILWAY PASSENGER SERVICES

The Minister of Transport having given approval under powers conferred by the Transport Act, 1962, the Scottish Region of British Railways announce the withdrawal of ALL railway passenger train services between ABERDEEN and BALLATER on and from MONDAY, 28th FEBRUARY, 1966

From the same date the following stations and halts will be closed to passenger traffic:—

CULTS	DEE STREET HALT	ABOYNE
CULTER	GLASSEL	DINNET
PARK	TORPHINS	CAMBUS O' MAY
CRATHES	LUMPHANAN	HALT
BANCHORY	DESS	BALLATER

The following alternative services by road passenger transport will be available:—

OPERATED BY:
MESSRS W. ALEXANDER & SONS (NORTHERN) LTD.

Table No.	Service No.	
1	1	ABERDEEN-BALLATER/BRAEMAR via Cults, Culter, Banchory, Aboyne, Dinnet and Crathie.
3	1B	ABERDEEN-GLEN O' DEE HOSPITAL.
4	1C	ABERDEEN-BANCHORY via Cults.
6	1E	BANCHORY-BALLATER via Glassel Station, Torphins, Lumphanan, Dess and Aboyne.
7	2	CULTER/KEPPLEHILLS/STONEYWOOD-DYCE.
21	14	ABERDEEN-ABOYNE via Torphins and Lumphanan.

These tables include certain additional services which are required by the Minister of Transport as a condition of consent to the withdrawal of the passenger train service.

A pamphlet giving full details of the alternative services will be available shortly at stations.

PARCELS TRAFFIC

Parcels and other passenger-rated Merchandise traffic will continue to be dealt with meantime at ABOYNE, BALLATER, BANCHORY and CULTER. Collection and delivery arrangements will be as follows:—

ABOYNE for BALLATER, DINNET, GLASSEL, LUMPHANAN and TORPHINS.

ABERDEEN for BANCHORY, CULTER, CRATHES, CULTS and PARK

Further information may be obtained from the Station Master at Aberdeen.

Newspaper announcement of the withdrawal of passenger services, 1966 up between the Deeside Railway Preservation Committee, the local MP and a number of private individuals on one hand, and British Railways Board and Ministry of Transport on the other.

The closure date was fixed for 26 February 1966, the BRB notice announcing 'the withdrawal of ALL railway passenger train services between ABERDEEN and BALLATER on and from MONDAY, 28th FEBRUARY, 1966'. Subsequently a petition protesting against the closure, and carrying 577 signatures, was lodged with the Minister but it was of no avail.

SERVICES WILL CEASE . . .

Saturday, 26 February saw the last day of passenger services on Deeside, and never in recent years had the trains been so crowded. It was customary for the line to be worked by a pair of two-car diesel multiple-units, but most of the trains that day were strengthened. The 8.09 am train from Aberdeen was a three-car unit which was well filled, but the 1.55 pm down was the busiest train of the day, with many Aberdeen families turning out for a last trip along Deeside in the afternoon sunshine.

At Ballater the station staff had their busiest day for years. Return tickets for the 12.30 train, coming back from Aberdeen at 1.30 pm, gave the station an all-time record, more than £25 worth being sold. Queues formed at the ticket office and barrier—a practically unheard-of situation at Ballater. Although the afternoon trains were crowded—perhaps because it was such a fine day—the last two scheduled trains were something of a disappointment. Only seventy people travelled from Aberdeen on the 8.35 pm (although thirty more saw them off) and the last timetable train from Ballater (the 8.35 pm) arrived in Aberdeen with only fifty-six passengers on board.

All along the line local people had turned out to watch these last trains, which crossed at Park. The down train arrived at Ballater to wild cheering from the crowd and a blast of its horn. This train was not to be left at the terminus but was brought back to Aberdeen by an Aberdeen crew and, as a last gesture, British Railways allowed enthusiasts to travel back on it, free of charge. Mr W. Stewart, the stationmaster, summoned the passengers with the century-old handbell and, to a broadside of detonators, the train pulled out of the station for the last time.

The remaining freight service did not last long. On Friday, 15 July 1966, the service was curtailed beyond Culter, and the stations at Banchory, Aboyne and Ballater completely closed. The down train, drawn by a Clayton Type 1 diesel, No D8610 (the first and last of this type to be seen on Deeside) stopped at Culter to pick up the travelling signalman. At Banchory there were two wagons to be shunted and at Auchlossan crossing the train stopped to enable the guard to open the 'gates', which consisted of two strands of barbed wire, each adorned with a piece of red cloth— the proper gates had been torn off a week before by a train failing to brake in time.

After a stop at Aboyne the train arrived at Ballater half-an-hour ahead of schedule, and was greeted by a crowd of about thirty, which had turned out to see its 'trainie' for the last time. After some shunting operations and lunch, the train left Ballater for the last time to repeated blasts of the engine's horn. For the return trip there was a large turnout of enthusiasts and residents along the lineside to wave the train on its way. One hour ahead of schedule the diesel arrived at Clayhills sidings at Aberdeen, at 3.45 pm.

Culter did not long remain the terminus of the Deeside Railway, for Friday, 30 December 1966, saw the final day of service on the line with the running of the last freight train and the closing of Culter station. The run was also notable in that it was the first steam train to be seen on the branch for some years. Permission had been given for a party of members of the Great North of Scotland Railway Association to travel on the train and some thirty members and friends purchased 1st class tickets at a charge of 6s 6d each for the return journey.

The train consisted of four BR standard brakevans hauled by a class 'B1' locomotive, No 61180. It was driven by Frank Duncan who had driven Deeside trains (including seven Royal trains) for the previous twenty-three years. The guard, Bob Taylor, was also an old Deeside man. At Culter the train pulled on into the goods sidings, where the engine ran round the brakevans, and back to collect seven wagons of timber. The train being made up, it returned to the passenger station, from where it set off on a fast non-stop run to Ferryhill with the engine running tender first. All along the line horses and cows in adjacent fields were seen running in fright from the strange smoking apparition, and people in their gardens and windows, and on lineside paths and roads, waved a last farewell to the Deeside Railway. The sun was shining down on the Dee valley that December day, the air was calm and clear and the ground was crisp underfoot.

Near Ferryhill Junction (where the line is still double) the points were set and locked for the last time. The line was closed. The Deeside token was handed back to the Ferryhill signalman for the last time and the train ran into Guild Street goods yard beside the tall freightliner gantries of the 'New Face of British Rail', which had no place for the Deeside.

At the time of writing (1967) all sidings and loops have been lifted, and the Minister of Transport has announced a new plan for British Railways under which social considerations will be taken into account when considering closures.

The Deeside line need not have been closed, but on Deeside 113 years, 3 months and 22 days of history have come to an end.

CHAPTER 7

Locomotives and Rolling-Stock

THE DEESIDE RAILWAY ENGINES

Before the railway opened, Mr Willett, the company's Engineer, went to Glasgow in May 1853 to view two tank engines that the Caledonian Railway had for sale, but nothing came of the affair and in June two tank engines were ordered from Hawthorn of Leith at a price of £1,500 each.

Later in the month, Mr Willett advised that the engines should be altered to give greater length, two more wheels, and larger capacity water tanks and this was agreed to, the price being adjusted to £1,625. A month later, a Mr Thomas Bouch of Edinburgh offered the company a profit of £100 on the price if they would release either or both for supply to another railway for which he was acting. The board agreed at first, as arrangements had been made for the Scottish Central Railway to provide its trains but, as has been recorded, this arrangement very quickly proved unsatisfactory and Hawthorn was urged to speed up the order. Only seven weeks after the line opened the annual general meeting was told that the directors had ordered two locomotives of their own: No 1 was delivered on 20 February 1844 and No 2 in the following August.

The two engines were o—4—2 tank locomotives and No 2 was to be the longest surviving Deeside Railway engine, not being withdrawn until twenty-nine years later. No 1 was sold for £800 to James Livesey of Cannon Street, London, in April 1865, being 'too light for traffic'.

No 3 was an entirely different type of engine, being bought readymade from Isaac Dodds & Sons of Rotherham. This locomotive was an o—4—2 tender type fitted with Dodds' patent wedge motion, and costing the company £2,111 19s od. It was delivered some time between May and August, 1854. The wedge motion was a most unsatisfactory arrangement and, as on other railways using this type of engine, a great deal of trouble was experienced with it. There was a tendency for the motion to seize up and render the engine completely immovable, and it seems unlikely that No 3 ever did very much work.

When the GNS took over the running of the Deeside line in 1866 No 3 was still on the books, although in the valuation report it was stated that 'in its present condition it is unserviceable'. It was later decided by the joint committee set up under the 1866 Act to 'sell No 3 for what it was worth and credit the Deeside Railway's Capital Account'. Although a report on GNS plant dated 10 September 1868 refers to No 3 Deeside engine as being 'partly broken up and unserviceable' it has been said that it was eventually bought by a Mr W. T. Wheatley. In previous accounts there has been confusion between No 1 and No 3, it being said that No 1 was broken up and No 3 sold to an agent for a Spanish company, but the actual position is as given above. No 3 was finally removed from the GNS stock list in 1868.

After this disastrous affair, the Deeside went back to Hawthorn whose engines they knew and trusted, and ordered from that company a tender engine, again an 0—4—2, which was delivered on 25 March 1857 and cost £2,250. It was given the number 4. This engine weighed about twenty-eight tons and had an open cab with only a front plate to protect the crew and a considerable front-end overhang. The tender was four-wheeled and weighed about sixteen tons. In service No 4 obviously proved satisfactory for it became the standard design on the line, the company eventually owning five of similar type.

Two further engines identical to No 4 were delivered in July 1859 and June 1860 and numbered 5 and 6. These cost £2,320 and £2,250 respectively, plus an extra £35 for steel tyres on No 6. No 5 was thus available for the opening of the Aboyne extension, the line now being too long for the limited capacity of the tank engines. In September of 1860 No 6, together with a quantity of rolling-stock, was transferred on paper to the Deeside Extension Railway, although in practice this made no difference as the two companies were virtually the same: it was transferred back again in April 1861. It has been suggested that there was a fourth Hawthorn 0—4—2, numbered 7 and delivered at the same time as No 5, but see Note (h) to the table.

In 1864, the need for more locomotive power was met by the purchase of a further identical engine, this time secondhand. In 1861 Hawthorn had built a locomotive of the 'Deeside type' for the Banff, Portsoy & Strathisla Railway and this was taken over in 1863 by the Great North. Renumbered 39 in the Great North's stock, it was sold by that system to the Deeside Railway for £2,100 and was numbered 7 in the Deeside stock. This engine is the subject of more widely-conflicting stories than practically any other in Scotland (see note [m] to the table).

The final engine, No 8, was similar to the other o—4—2s but slightly larger. Delivered in June 1866 ready for the opening to Ballater, it was equipped with a twenty-four-ton six-wheel tender to enable it to run Royal trains non-stop from Aberdeen, and cost £2,478 18s od delivered.

The Deeside livery was smart, the engines being painted dark blue, with black bands and lining on the tender and cabsides. Here again there are discrepancies. Some of the engines—for example No 4—had a panel on the cabside carrying the number and the legend 'Deeside Railway' but, while Vallance claims that this was in gilt, the SLS *Journal* (reference [f] to the table) states that it was white. In view of the Victorian love of ostentation, the former seems more probable.

The livery adopted for No 2, one of the original tank engines, is reputed to have been tartan for a time. Once again, firm details are practically impossible to obtain. The story is that No 2 was delegated to work the first messenger trains—the Queen's specials —and for this duty was painted all over in the Royal Stuart Dress tartan, a striking pattern of almost equally prominent reds, whites, blues and greens.

Vallance compromises by saying that the tartan was confined to panels on the sides of the tanks, but in view of Queen Victoria's love of tartan (at that time Balmoral Castle had tartan soft furnishings virtually throughout) and the precedent of an earlier engine of the North British Railway that is known to have been painted all over in the Stuart tartan (see Hamilton Ellis' *Four Main Lines*, 1950, Ian Allan), there is no reason to doubt that this was the case on Deeside also. A bonny sight it must have made, but it is said that the directors soon changed their minds and had No 2 repainted in the quieter red hues of the MacDuff tartan.

Although no further proof of the use of a tartan livery has come to light, the story seems to have originated in some early notes by the late Major S. A. Forbes, which were passed on by him to Sir Malcolm Barclay-Harvey, in whose book it was first published.

Under The Great North of Scotland Railway (Amalgamation) Act of 1866, the Great North leased the Deeside company, but was

DEESIDE RAILWAY

Deeside No	Date delivered	GNS Number (h)	Date withdrawn	Type	Driving wheels
1	Feb 1854	—	1865 1866 (a)	o—4—2T	5 ft o in (b) *or* 4 ft 6 in (g)
2	Aug 1854	39	1883 (d, e) (May 1884) (a, b)	o—4—2T	5 ft o in (b) *or* 4 ft 6 in (g)
3	1854 (Mar 1857) (f)	49(j)	1868 (c, j) (1866) (f) (1864) (b, d)	o—4—2	5 ft o in (b, d) *or* 4 ft 6 in (g)
4	Mar 1857	50	1875		
5	Jly 1859	51	1876	o—4—2	5 ft o in (d) *or* 4 ft 6 in (b, c, g)
6	Jun 1860	52	1878		
7	1864 (1863) (b)	53	Dec 1879 (Dec 1880) (f)	o—4—2	5 ft o in *or* 4 ft 6 in (c, g)
8	1866	54	Dec 1880	o—4—2	5 ft o in *or* 4 ft 6 in (c, g)

REFERENCES:

(a) Allchin, M. C. V. *Locomotives of the Great North of Scotland Railway*, 1950

(b) Barclay-Harvey, C. M. *A History of the Great North of Scotland Railway*, 2nd Edn

(c) Craven, E. *Notes on G.N.S.R. Locomotives, compiled from the Minutes of the Directors' Meetings*

(d) Vallance, H. A. *The Great North of Scotland Railway*, 1965

(e) Vallance, H. A. 'The Deeside Railway', *Railway Magazine*, Feb, 1957

(f) Stephenson Locomotive Society *Journal*, Sept, 1954

(g) G.N.S.R.A. Abstract No 7, 'Locomotive Classification and Numbering', 1966, as amended, 1968

(h) This numbering is according to recent research by Craven (c). Hitherto, most authorities have copied Barclay-Harvey (b), who claimed that the ex-BP & SR engine was numbered 3, to replace the original No 3 by Dodds, and that a further o—4—2 tender engine, numbered 7 and identical to 4, 5, and 6 existed, which was supplied in November 1859 and withdrawn in 1877. According to this, the re-numbering was thus:

LOCOMOTIVES

Cylinders	Builder	Notes
13 in x 16 in (b) or 13 in x 18 in (e, g) i.c.	Hawthorn	
13 in x 16 in (b) or 13 in x 18 in (g) i.c.	Hawthorn	
13 in x 18 in (g) or 14¼ in x 22 in (c) i.c.	Dodds & Son	? tank (a, b, f)
15¼ in x 24 in (c) or 15 in x 24 in (g) or 16 in x 22 in (d) o.c.	Hawthorn	(k)
15½ in x 24 in (c) or 15 in x 24 in (g) or 16 in x 22 in (d) o.c.	Hawthorn (Vulcan) (m)	Ex-BP & SR engine (m)
15¼ in x 24 in (c) or 15 in x 24 in (g) or 16 in x 22 in (d) o.c.	Hawthorn	6-wheel tender ? tank engine (a)

REFERENCES :

DEESIDE :   2   3*   4   5   6   7   8
G.N.S.R. :   39   40   49   50   51   52   53
                    * Ex-BP & SR

Vallance (d) says that 40 and 53 in this scheme of numbering were subsequently re-numbered 63 and 64 respectively, in 1878

(j) According to Craven (c) this engine was taken over, but broken up before it received its number

(k) The S.L.S. *Journal* (f) claim that Deeside No 4 was the ex-BP & SR engine

(m) There are several versions of the history of this engine. References a and b claim that it was BP & SR No 4, while references c, d, and g claim that it was BP & SR No 3. References a, b, d, and f claim that the BP & SR bought it secondhand while references c, and g (based on modern research of original records) state that it was bought direct from Hawthorn, the maker. References a, b, d, and f claim that it was built by Vulcan Foundry, Warrington. References b, c, f, and g state that BP & SR No 4 was named *Strathisla* and that No 3 was named *Keith*, while references a, and d, claim that the names were the reverse of this required to maintain the rolling-stock as 'a separate and distinct Plant' and to continue to have it 'marked and lettered with the Name of the Deeside Railway Company'. It was not until the amalgamation of 1876 that the locomotives became the property of the Great North and could legally be renumbered into its stock, but the literature abounds with references to the renumbering of these engines taking place in 1866-7 subsequent to the lease, and it seems probable that this was done despite the provisions of the 1866 Act. The actual renumbering scheme adopted is, like much of the history of these engines, subject to alternative stories. The two schemes which have been quoted are both given in the table and Note (h) appended to it.

When the joint committee set up to arrange the lease considered the locomotives it obtained an independent valuation by Connor of the Caledonian Railway. The inventory, including both this valuation and the classification of Cowan of the Great North, appears in the Deeside minute book of 30 September 1869, and makes interesting reading.

Cowan's Classification December 1867		Connor's valuation			
Deeside No	GNS No	First cost	Miles run	Deprec'n*	Present value
2	39	£1,625	200,052	£928 16s	£696 4s
3	49	Unserviceable			
4	50	£2,383	161,581	£1,111	£1,283
5	51	£2,300	132,264	£869	£1,431
6	52	£2,405	121,704	£836 5s	£1,568
7	53	£2,100	65,666	£273 19s	£1,826
8	54	£2,492	22,561	£160 13s	£2,331 7s

* Based on an assumed total life of 350,000 miles

NB. The small differences in price between Connor's figures and those recorded earlier probably represent the difference between basic cost and total 'delivered' price paid to include tools, etc.

THE GREAT NORTH ENGINES

When the Great North took over the Deeside line the old 0—4—2s continued in service for a while but as they became worn out they were replaced by Great North engines. The Great North was notable in that, after the first few years, all its tender engines were of the 4—4—0 arrangement. Apart from nine tank engines the company never owned any six-coupled engines, nor did it ever

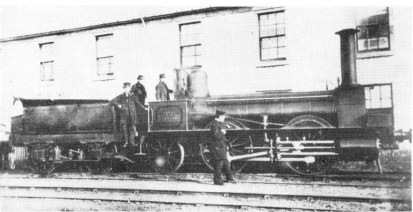

Page 127 : THE DEESIDE RAILWAY'S 0—4—2 HAWTHORN LOCOMOTIVES
(42) *Identity unknown (? No 7)*
(43) *No 4*
(44) *Ex-Deeside locomotive* (GNS *No* 51) *at Banchory*

Page 128: STEAM LOCOMOTION

(45) GNS *No* 33 *at Dinnet*
(46) *The original Culter Mills 'Puggy'*

have any single-drivers at all despite their widespread popularity elsewhere.

The story of the Great North's engines has been told elsewhere in fairly great detail and will not be repeated here. The first Great North design to appear on Deeside was Cowan's 'L' class followed by his 'C' class. Manson's handsome 4—4—0s also served on the line and it was he who was responsible for the only class of six-coupled engines which the Great North ever owned, the classes 'D' and 'E' 0—6—0 side tank engines that worked the suburban services for so many years.

Johnson also introduced a class of tank engines, the 0—4—4 class 'R' which took over the 'subby' services and ran them with smartness and distinction for over forty years. Pickersgill's classes 'T' and 'V' also distinguished themselves on Deeside. The two steam railcars which the Great North used as an experiment in 1905-6 spent a brief and unsuccessful period on the suburban services, and after the 1914-18 war Heywood's handsome class 'F' also did excellent service on the line.

The livery of Great North engines was a striking shade of grass green with darker green edging and lining-out in black and red. The cylinders were black and the wheels green. Until 1876, the numbers were painted on the splashers but thereafter oval plates with raised letters and figures were attached to the cabsides.

During the war Heywood made a change in livery, painting the wheels black without any lining, and in 1917 an all-black livery was adopted with yellow and red lining. The last eight engines of class 'F' had the Great North coat of arms on the front splasher and, above this, a curved nameplate conforming to the splasher's contour.

THE LNE AND BR STEAM ENGINES

At the time of grouping in 1923, the LNE took over 122 engines from the Great North and, for many years, there were few changes, the Great North engines being well-built and well-maintained so that few saw less than forty years' service and many lasted for more than fifty. The only two 'foreign' types which did become familiar on Deeside were the 'B12's and 'B1's. The 'B12' class of 4—6—0s were designed by S. D. Holden for the Great Eastern Railway in 1911 and, when they were displaced, were found ideal, with their relatively high power and low axle loadings, for the Great North system.

The 'B1' 4—6—0s were introduced to the area in 1946. Built by

H

Thompson during the second world war, they had slightly smaller driving wheels (6 ft 2 in) and cylinders (20 in x 26 in) than the 'B12's but were heavier than the older engines and capable of a greater tractive effort.

The LNE livery was apple green and, after grouping, the engines on Deeside reverted to the old familiar green in place of Heywood's black. In 1928 the LNE itself reverted to black for all but the most powerful classes and only black steam engines ran on the Deeside line thereafter.

In early British Railways days the 'B1's remained the main source of motive power but, when the BR standard designs began to appear, some of the '4 MT' class of 2—6—4 tanks were allocated to Deeside.

Under nationalisation, a variety of locomotive types found themselves on strange metals and from time to time unusual 'foreign' engines such as ex-North British 'J36' 0—6—0s and Stanier 'black-fives' were seen on the Deeside line.

The last steam engine to run on the line was a 'B1' No 61180, which hauled the last train to Culter and back (more than seven years after diesel and electric traction had taken over) on 30 December 1966.

THE CULTER MILLS ENGINES

Round about the turn of the century the Culter Paper Mills Company felt a need for a railway within its premises and accordingly lines were laid and an electric vehicle acquired. Unfortunately, no records have survived as to what type of equipment was supplied, but it is said to have been an 'electric trolley' taking its power from overhead cables.

With the increased turnover of the next twenty years, the provision of a locomotive became necessary to handle the goods trucks. In 1920 an 0—4—0 outside-cylinder saddle-tank was purchased from Peckett & Sons Limited of Bristol. One of a common and very popular design, the engine had the works number 1548 and was painted green. It carried a brass plate on the nearside of the cab with THE CULTER MILLS PAPER CO. LIMITED engraved on it. This engine gave excellent service for thirty-two years until it was replaced in 1952 by a secondhand example of the same type and make, bought from a company in the north of England. This second engine was built in 1941 and had the works number 1998: it, too, was painted green, with red frame and buffer beams, and the brass owner's plate was transferred to it. Because of a variety of reasons the amount of freight carried to and from the works by rail declined, road transport taking over much of it, and the Culter 'puggy' ended its days rusting in its shed.

DIESEL AND ELECTRIC TRACTION

In 1958, British Railways began an experiment on Deeside which cost £50,000 to set up and was unique in this country. In collaboration with the North of Scotland Hydro-Electric Board, Bruce Peebles Limited, and Chloride Batteries Limited, a battery-powered electric railcar was introduced to the Deeside line. Converted at Cowlairs works from a 1956 Derby-built two-car diesel multiple-unit, the railcar had seating for thirty-one first-class and eighty-six second-class passengers.

The batteries were charged at special charging plants at Aberdeen and Ballater, with a short charge at the end of each trip and a complete recharge overnight at the off-peak rates of only $\frac{1}{4}$d a unit. The charging equipment was 3 phase, 50 cycles ac, operating at 6,600 volts at Aberdeen and 11,000 volts at Ballater.

The two-car unit (Nos SC 79998 and SC 79999) was initially scheduled to perform three runs a day in each direction and was notable for its smooth and silent running. Although having a top designed speed of 60 mph, the set was limited to 50 mph because of track restrictions. It was withdrawn from Deeside in August 1962 following a series of breakdowns and minor fires and was replaced by a diesel multiple-unit.

At the same time as the battery electric railcar was introduced, a diesel multiple-unit was also put on the line. Initially this was a secondhand Metropolitan-Cammel unit brought in from further south in the region, but later it was replaced by a Craven two-car unit consisting of a motor-brake second and a driving-trailer composite car, with twelve first-class and 103 second-class seats.

The Deeside freight services were also hauled by diesel traction in their later years. The run (scheduled as trip A9) was rostered officially to a Class 1,000 hp diesel locomotive and this was usually a 72½ ton North British Type 2 diesel-electric 1,000 bhp Bo-Bo— the same class that also generally hauled the royal trains. Occasionally 72 ton English Electric Type 1 1,000 bhp Bo-Bo locomotives performed the turn. On 15 July 1966 the last train to run to Ballater—a freight train—was hauled by the only Clayton Type 1 (900 bhp Bo-Bo) ever to be seen on the line, No D 8610. In the last five and a half months of freight operation, when the service ran only as far as Culter, a 47 ton British Railways o—6—o 350 bhp diesel-electric shunter was employed for this duty.

ROLLING-STOCK

Very few details and no illustrations have survived of the early Deeside coaches; they were four-wheelers and described as being constructed with 'solid material and workmanship'. The maker was Brown Marshall & Company of Birmingham. There was a railed-in top for luggage and parcels and a railed-in seat and footboard for the conductor, set at each end, after the fashion of the ordinary horse-drawn coach. The third-class coaches were open from end to end, without partitions, and passengers could climb over the narrow (and bare) seats to join an acquaintance further along the carriage. The doors were narrow and fitted with unpadded sliding windows which are said to have 'rattled disagreeably'. The solitary lamp was supported in the fork of an iron support extending from the centre seat to the roof.

The improved facilities provided for first-class passengers (neither the Deeside nor the Great North ever used second-class accommodation) included the division of the coach into three compartments, with upholstered seats and backs, and the fitting of window blinds. Cavities were provided in the floor of smoking compartments to hold spittoons, but there was no attempt to provide heating in winter. The guards' vans were externally very similar to the passenger coaches but in the roof at one end was a 'cupola' or 'dovecote' about three feet higher than the rest of the coach and fitted with windows all round so that the guard could continue his 'roof duties' while inside.

These coaches were in use for very many years, and were later supplemented by similar stock from the Great North at the time of the takeover. The Deeside Railway is said to have painted its coaching stock blue, in similar fashion to the locomotives. When the line opened the company owned no goods wagons but some were quickly obtained and later the company made its own at the workshops at Banchory, a practice that was still continuing at the takeover.

In Great North days the first improvement was the introduction of Manson's six-wheel coaches, and these were followed in 1898 by Pickersgill's bogie corridor composite coaches which were first built for the Aberdeen—Inverness main line. Two of these coaches were included in the make-up of the Deeside Express from that year and, in 1906, a new type of composite coach was introduced which had three first and three third compartments, the centre one of each running the full width of the carriage, and corridors going to the ends on opposite sides, with a toilet at each end. Thereafter, coaching stock continued to improve with the years and calls for little comment, the Deeside line receiving the usual branch-line assortment of main-line cast-offs.

In the 1890s trials were made with the Westinghouse brake system and this proved so satisfactory that in 1891 it was adopted as standard. One further unusual aspect of Great North coaching practice was that gas lighting was never used. After 1896, the old oil lamps were gradually replaced by electric lighting on Stone's system.

The Great North originally painted its coaching stock a sombre brown that has been variously described as dull brown, pale chocolate, and lake, but in the 1890s Pickersgill introduced a much more attractive scheme, the lower panels being purple lake, and the upper panels cream, picked out with red and yellow. Wagon stock was painted dark grey, although the open wagons were originally painted dark red and this colour continued in use for brakevans and departmental wagons until 1922.

One entirely unique vehicle built by the Great North and used on the Deeside line was its Royal saloon. Originally built by Pickersgill at Kittybrewster as a saloon for hire to special parties and for the use of the directors, the carriage was forty-eight feet long, cost £1,735 6s 11d, and was entered in the stock list on 21 September 1898 as Saloon No 1. In 1902 it was upgraded to a Royal saloon and thus became the only royal carriage ever owned by a pre-grouping Scottish railway.

Although the length of the saloon was the same as that of the bogie composites built at the same time it looked unlike any other Great North carriage as it had a clerestory roof. Steam heating and electric lighting were installed and the layout comprised a servants' compartment, a first-class compartment, a drawing-room (which could be converted for night use) and a smokeroom. The saloon was panelled throughout in walnut, mahogany and oak in a most attractive style. After the death of King Edward VII the saloon reverted to its original role and was not withdrawn until 1964, having suffered only minor structural alterations. It is now preserved by the Scottish Railway Preservation Society and is to be restored to its original livery.

CHAPTER 8

Conclusions

When the first prospectus for a Deeside railway was issued nearly a century and a quarter ago the line was envisaged as having three main functions—to carry timber and other freight, to provide what is now known as a commuter service, and to act as a tourist route. To the end these functions remained the same, the very last train to run on the line carrying both tourists and timber, as had the earliest trains. Why then did the line fail?

One must first look at what the coming of the railway brought about. Designed originally to link already existing townships along the Dee valley with Aberdeen, there inevitably grew up other communities along the line, fed by it and supported by it. In particular, Torphins, Lumphanan and Dinnet were peculiarly dependent on the railway for their development and continued growth. In addition, such older centres as Banchory, Aboyne and Ballater received a new lease of life from the railway, both as holiday resorts and, latterly, as commuting areas for Aberdeen. Inevitably, with the development of motor transport, the railways felt the effects of competition.

In one half-yearly report of the GNS it was noted that a signalman at Kintore had reported seeing four motor cars pass in one day, all carrying four people: the chairman explained how very serious this would be if four motor cars carrying sixteen people every day took that traffic off the railways. It has indeed been suggested that the Great North laid the seeds of its own destruction by the introduction of motor bus services, but this is clearly not so, as if the railway company had not done so, others would have.

Despite the competition of road services the railway should have been able to compete effectively. Much of the route lay in highland areas which are annually under snow and ice for several months of the year. In the survey that was made for the Beeching report it was shown that, on typical winter weekdays, some 260-280 passengers used the line. Were it not for the fare structure and the total lack of salesmanship, the numbers in the summer season should have risen way above this with the tourist traffic, but in fact they were substantially the same. Every year some 750,000 people visit Aberdeen, and only half of these bring cars with them, so that the potential was enormous. Basically, the line lost money because no efforts were made to increase traffic which, in a tourist area such as Deeside, was obviously there to be tapped.

Now the railway is closed. The area within the Banchory-Torphins-Lumphanan-Aboyne 'loop' is slowly dying for want of an adequate transport service while the rails are rusting and becoming overgrown with weeds; station buildings are becoming derelict; children play on the track. It has been suggested that when the rails are eventually lifted the track bed could remain as a hiker's route into the highlands. Perhaps, if trains are not to run along Deeside again, this could be the line's final best memorial. One imagines that Queen Victoria, who herself loved the Deeside highlands so much, would have approved.

LAMENT

(Tune: *The Londonderry Air*)

On Deeside rail, beside the singing river,
    The 'Sputnik' ran (the little Deeside train),
And culled at morn commuters bound for Aberdeen,
    And in the evening brought them home again,
'Tis three long years since Dr Beeching (now my Lord),
    Proclaimed in print the Deeside train must go,
Because he said the bus was more efficient,
    Especially on roads agleam with hard-packed snow.

Oh Sputnik Train, I still can hear your 'toot-a-hoot',
    The salmon leap above the surging Dee,
The children gather, rustling bags of tattie-crisps,
    And you, dear train, were waiting here for me.
But now we stand, growing colder, ever colder,
    The bus is late, and faster falls the snow,
But I will write and tell you what I think of you,
    Oh Barbara, oh Barbara, I hate you so!

(Mrs R. E. Innes of Learney, Torphins)

Appendixes

1: STATION MILEAGES AND OPENING AND CLOSING DATES

	Miles	Opened	Closed to passengers (as and from)	Closed to freight (where different)
Aberdeen Joint Stn	0	2– 8–1854		
Ferryhill Junction	0⅝	8– 9–1853	1– 8–1854	—
Holburn Street	1⅜	2– 7–1894	5– 4–1937	—
Ruthrieston	1¾	1856	5– 4–1937	—
Pitfodels	3	2– 7-1894	5– 4–1937	—
Cults	3⅝	8– 9–1853	28– 2–1966	15– 6–1964
West Cults	4⅛	1– 8–1894	5– 4–1937	—
Bieldside	4¾	1– 6–1897	5– 4–1937	—
Murtle	5⅜	8– 9–1853	5– 4–1937	—
Milltimber	6¼	1854	5– 4–1937	—
Culter	7⅜	8– 9–1853	28– 2–1966	2– 1–1967
Drum	9¾	1854	10– 9–1951	—
Park	10¾	8– 9–1853	28– 2–1966	15– 6–1964
Mills of Drum	12⅜	8– 9–1853	1– 1–1863	—
Crathes	14¼	1– 1–1863	28– 2–1966	15– 6–1964
Banchory	16¾	8– 9–1853	28– 2–1966	18– 7–1966
Dee St Halt	17½	6– 2–1961	28– 2–1966	—
Glassel	21⅜	2–12–1859	28– 2–1966	15– 6–1964
Torphins	23¾	2–12–1859	28– 2–1966	3–1965
Lumphanan	26⅞	2–12–1859	28– 2–1966	15– 6–1964
Dess	29½	2–12–1859	28– 2–1966	1– 7–1960
Aboyne	32¼	2–12–1859	28– 2–1966	18– 7–1966
Dinnet	36¾	17–10–1866	28– 2–1966	15– 6–1964
Cambus O'May	39⅜	1876	28– 2–1966	—
Ballater	43¼	17–10–1866	28– 2–1966	18– 7–1966

2: STATION LAYOUT DIAGRAMS; BASED ON THE
ORDNANCE SURVEY 25,000 SERIES,
EDITION OF 1901-03

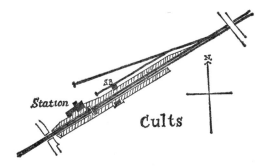

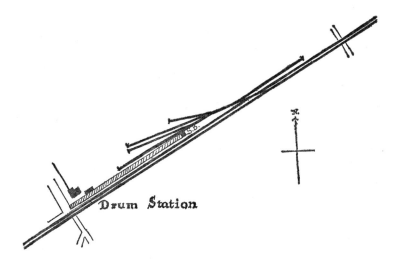

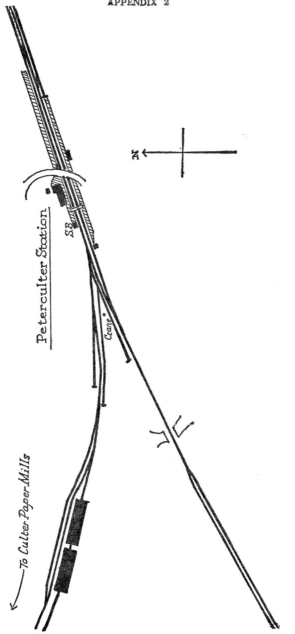

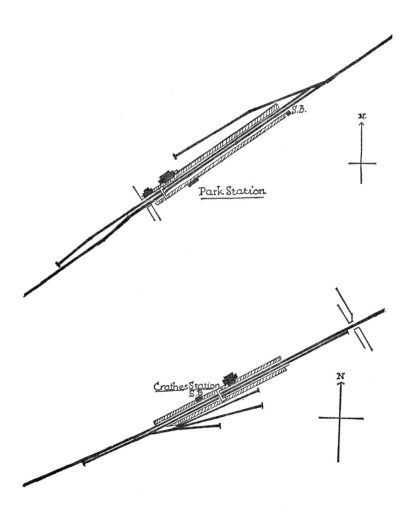

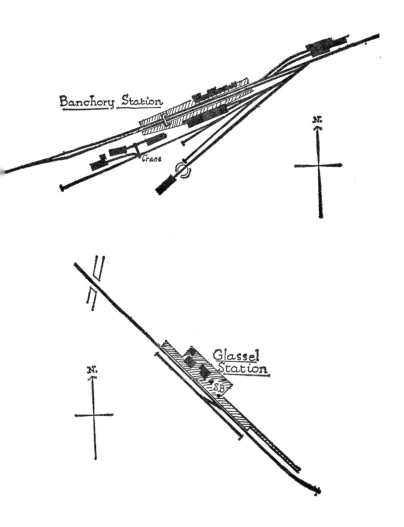

Banchory Station

Crane

N.

Glassel
Station

SB

N.

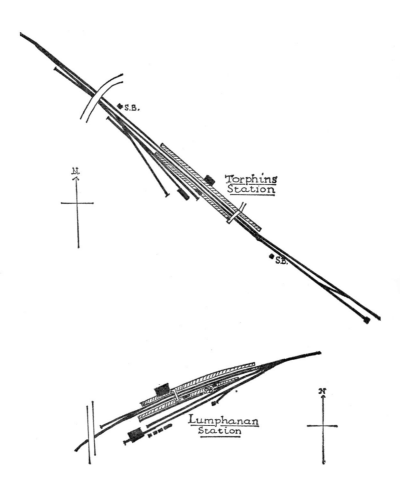

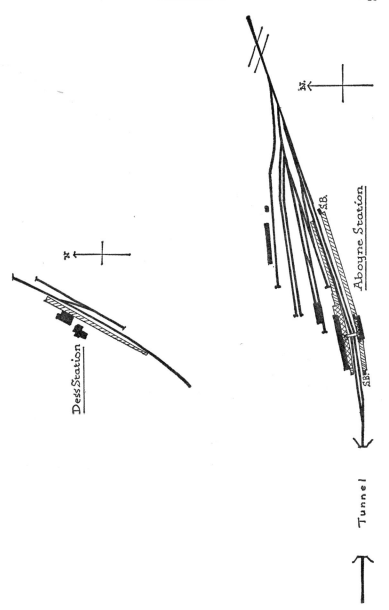

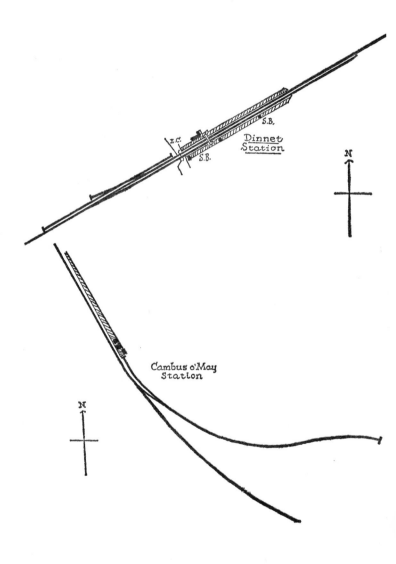

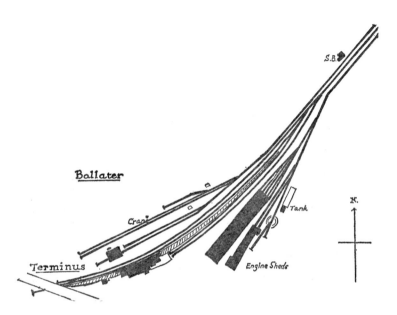

Ballater

Crane

Terminus

S.B.

Tank

Engine Sheds

N.

I

3: LAYOUT OF TYPICAL STATION BUILDING (CRATHES)

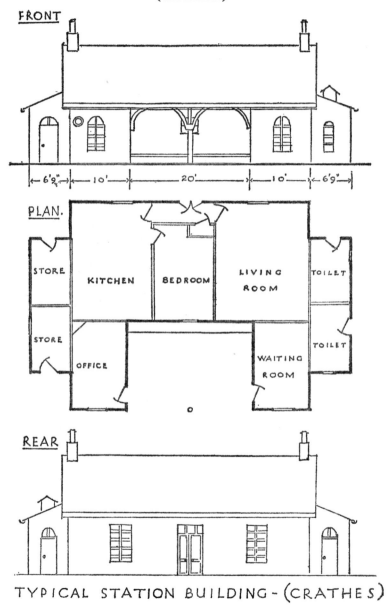

FRONT

PLAN.

REAR

TYPICAL STATION BUILDING - (CRATHES)

WEST END

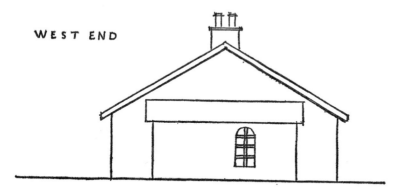

EAST END

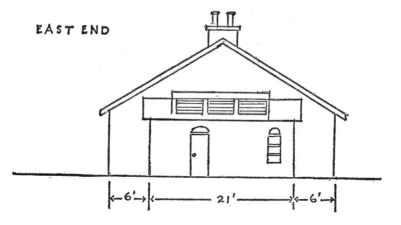

4: PROVISION OF DOUBLE TRACK

Track doubled

Ferryhill to West Cults	14 June 1884
West Cults to Murtle	13 July 1892
Murtle to Culter	24 September 1892
Culter to Park	28 August 1899

Track singled

Ferryhill to Park	2 December 1951

5: LENGTH OF PASSING LOOPS

Under British Railways the length of passing loops was assessed in terms of the number of 'standard wagons' (excluding engine and brakevan) that could be used in making up a freight train. For this purpose the equivalent number of wagons was calculated thus:

All types of bogie vehicles	3 wagons
All other long wheelbase vehicles	$1\frac{1}{2}$ wagons
Four-wheel mineral wagons of more than 16 tons capacity	$1\frac{1}{4}$ wagons
All other types of wagon	1 wagon

The overall length limit on the Deeside line was forty-five wagons. Individual length limits were:

Culter	34 wagons
Park	34 wagons
Banchory	44 wagons
Torphins	45 wagons
Lumphanan	19 wagons
Aboyne	33 wagons
Dinnet	23 wagons

6: POSITIONING OF MANSON'S AUTOMATIC TOKEN EXCHANGE APPARATUS

Signalbox	For down trains	For up trains
Ferryhill Junction	—	N end of signalbox
Culter	Opposite signalbox	Opposite ,, ,,
Park	,, ,, ,,	,, ,, ,,
Banchory	8 yd W of ,, ,,	8 yd W of ,, ,,
Torphins	68 yd E ,, ,, ,,	Opposite ,, ,,
Lumphanan	57 yd E ,, ,, ,,	57 yd E of ,, ,,
Aboyne	5 yd W ,, ,, ,,	Opposite ,, ,,
Dinnet	20 yd W ,, ,, ,,	20 yd W of ,, ,,

7: LIST OF ROYAL TRAINS KNOWN TO HAVE BEEN PROVIDED BY THE GREAT NORTH OF SCOTLAND RAILWAY

Date		Journey	Provided for
1902 Sep	8	Invergordon to Ballater	King Edward VII and Queen Alexandra
„	16	Ballater to Dalmeny	Queen Alexandra
„	26	Ballater to Fochabers	Prince of Wales
1903 Sep	7	King's Cross to Ollerton	King Edward VII
„	8	Ollerton-Doncaster	King Edward VII
	-10	(return each day)	
„	14	Ollerton to Ballater	King Edward VII
1906 Aug 27		Advie to Ballater	Prince of Wales
Sep 27		Ballater to Holburn St and Aberdeen to Ballater	King Edward VII and Queen Alexandra
1907 Aug 23		Ballater to Dundee	Queen Alexandra
1908 Aug 24		Ballater to Dundee	Queen Alexandra
1909 Aug 26		Ballater to Dundee	Queen Alexandra
1910 Sep 19		Ballater to Dundee	Queen Alexandra

8 (I): DOWN TRAIN, ABERDEEN—DINNET

Date: 8 April 1906
Train: 8.05 ex Aberdeen
Weather: Good
Engine: No 68

Dist (Miles)		Sch (min)	Actual m s	Stops m s	Speeds mph
—	Aberdeen Jnt Stn —				
3¾	Cults	(pass)	7.37		27.5
7½	Culter	14	4.58	1.10	48.9
9¾	Drum	6	4.59	0.13	27.1
10¾	Park	3	2.41	0.36	22.3
14¼	Crathes	6	5.30	0.30	38.1
16¾	Banchory	9	5.01	3.42	30.0
21¼	Glassel	10	9.21	0.24	28.8
23¾	Torphins	7	4.57	0.59	30.3
27	Lumphanan	8	7.22	0.37	26.4
29½	Dess	5	4.12	0.35	30.8
32¼	Aboyne	7	4.46	1.33	34.6
36¾	Dinnet	10	8.41		31.1
	Total times	85	70.05	10.19	
			80	24	

8 (II and III): UP TRAINS, DINNET—ABERDEEN

		II				III			
Run No		II				III			
Date		29 August 1906				18 September 1906			
Train		Deeside Express (8.40 ex-Dinnet)				6.26 am ex-Aboyne			
Load		Five 6-wheelers and two 8-wheelers				Eight 6-wheelers and one LNW 8-wheel Royal saloon			
Weather		Dry, no wind				Fine			
Engine		No 98				No 109			
Dist		Sch	Actual	Stops	Speeds	Sch	Actual	Stops	Speeds
Miles		Min	m s	m s	mph	Min	m s	m s	mph
	Dinnet	—				—			
4½	Aboyne	6	7.19	0.31	36.9				
7¼	Dess	pass	5.26		30.4	6	5.02		
9¾	Lumphanan	pass	3.38		41.3	6	5.19	0.20	29.6
13	Torphins	14	4.20	0.38	45.0	7	7.08	0.58	26.2
15½	Glassel	pass	3.46		39.8	5	3.11	0.18	44.9
20	Banchory	11	5.05	2.55	53.1	10	6.44	3.19	41.2
22½	Crathes	4	4.42	0.27	31.9	5	5.04	0.12	29.6
26	Park	pass	5.15		40.0	pass	5.15		40.0
27	Drum	pass	1.09		50.7	pass	0.58		62.1
29¼	Culter	pass	2.28		54.7	10	2.42	0.30	51.5
30½	Milltimber	pass	1.10		64.3	pass	2.45		26.1
31½	Murtle	pass	1.09		52.2	4	1.32	0.20	34.6
32	Bieldside	pass	0.47		38.3	pass	1.53		19.9
32⅝	W. Cults					pass	0.40		56.2
33¼	Cults	pass	1.17		58.4	4	1.11	0.44	29.9
33¾	Pitfodels	pass	0.33		54.5	pass	1.32		24.5
35	Ruthrieston	pass	1.28		51.1	pass	1.41		44.6
35½	Holburn St	(SC)	1.25	0.12	21.2		0.42	4.10	28.1
36¼	Aberdeen Jnt Stn	22	4.10		18.0	11	4.00		16.9
	Total times	57	55.07	2.43		68	57.19	10.51	
			57	50			68	10	

8 (IV): UP TRAIN, ABOYNE—ABERDEEN

	Date	24 September 1909
	Train	King's Messenger. 4.36 pm ex-Aboyne
	Load	Three 6-wheelers and one 4-wheeler
	Weather	Misty. Icy near Aberdeen
	Engine	No 14 (Manson 4—4—0, with 8-wheel tender)

Dist Miles		Sch Min	Actual m s	Stops m s	Speed mph
—	Aboyne				
2¾	Dess	pass	6.10		26.8
5¼	Lumphanan	pass	3.53		38.6
8½	Torphins	14	3.57	0.35	49.4
11	Glassel	pass	3.30		42.9
15½	Banchory	10	5.15	5.48	51.4
18	Crathes	6	4.50	0.12	31.0
21½	Park	pass	5.10		40.6
22½	Drum	pass	1.10		51.4
24¾	Culter	pass	2.25		55.9
26	Milltimber	pass	1.05		69.0
27	Murtle	pass	1.10		51.4
27½	Bieldside	pass	0.50		36.0
28⅛	W. Cults	pass	0.32		70.3
28¾	Cults	pass	0.41		54.4
29¼	Pitfodels	pass	0.27		66.6
30½	Ruthrieston	pass	1.37		27.8
31	Holburn St		0.50	1.28	36.0
	Ferryhill Jnctn	(SC)		4.29	
32¼	Aberdeen Jnt Stn		5.06		
	Total times		48.38	12.32	
			61	10	

9: OFFICERS BEFORE AMALGAMATION

DEESIDE RAILWAY

Chairmen		1846–9	Thomas Blaikie
		1849–75	John Duncan
		1875–6	Patrick Davidson
Secretaries		1846–9	William Leslie
		1849–76	William B. Ferguson
General Manager		1849–66	William B. Ferguson
Engineers		1846–9	William Cubitt
		1849–64	John Willet
		1864–6	William B. Ferguson
Locomotive Superintendents		1854–60	David Dean
		1860–6	Hugh Dean

ABOYNE & BRAEMAR RAILWAY

Chairman		1865–76	James Farquharson
Secretary		1865–6	William B. Ferguson

10: DIVIDENDS PAID BEFORE AMALGAMATION

	Deeside Railway Co %		Deeside Railway Extension Co %		Aboyne & Braemar Railway Co %
1854	5				
55	5				
56	5				
57	5				
58	5				
59	6				
60	6		2		
61	6		0		
62	$7\frac{1}{4}$		0		
63	7		2		
64	7		2		
65	7		2		
66	7		$2\frac{3}{4}$		
67	$7\frac{1}{2}$	guaranteed	3		0*
68	$7\frac{1}{2}$	,,	3	guaranteed	2
69	$7\frac{1}{2}$	,,	3	,,	2
70	$7\frac{1}{2}$	,,	3	,,	2
71	$7\frac{1}{2}$	,,	3	,,	2
72	$7\frac{1}{2}$	,,	3	,,	3
73	$7\frac{1}{2}$	,,	3	,,	$2\frac{1}{2}$
74	$7\frac{1}{2}$	,,	3	,,	$2\frac{1}{4}$
75	$7\frac{1}{2}$	,,	3	,,	$2\frac{1}{4}$
76	$9\frac{1}{4}$	,,	6	,,	$2\frac{1}{2}$
77	$9\frac{1}{2}$	,,	$6\frac{1}{4}$	,,	
78	$9\frac{3}{4}$	,,	$6\frac{1}{4}$	,,	
79	10	,,	$6\frac{3}{4}$	,,	

* After 3 months' working only

Author's Notes

This book has been based on original research into contemporary reports and documents. Most of the general information has been taken from the local press and all dates that are recorded and all information that is given which differs from that previously published have been at least double, often triple, checked against independent sources. Details concerning parliamentary legislation have been taken from the original Bills and Acts at first hand. Details concerning the original Deeside and Aboyne & Braemar railway companies have also been obtained from the companies' minute books. Train services have been checked against working and public timetables for the whole period of the line's existence.

Three items call for particular comment.

1. The numbering of the locomotives of the Deeside Railway Company differs from that previously published and is based on research by E. Craven. The present details agree with the minutes of the company's Traffic & Finance Committee and have been independently checked against the minute books by the author.

2. The date of Queen Victoria's first use of Ballater station differs from that previously suggested, but the new date has been triple-checked from independent sources and no confirmation of the previously suggested date has been found.

3. While it has been often suggested that Queen Victoria was responsible for the line not extending beyond the Gairn water, the proof presented in this book of an agreement (quoted in the directors' minutes), with the Queen's private solicitor is the first published confirmation of this.

Acknowledgments

The bulk of the material in this book has been prepared from contemporary accounts and records, and for access to the majority of these I am especially indebted to the staff of the Local and Commercial sections of Aberdeen Central Library, who have gone out of their way to help me in tracing and working on this material. Mr R. M. Hogg, Curator of Historical Records, British Railways Board, Edinburgh, and his staff have also been extremely helpful in providing access to a great deal of original material. The O'Dell collection of railway documents and cuttings is one of the richest hitherto untapped sources of information in the country and I am indebted to the librarian of King's College Library, Aberdeen, and his staff for access to the relevant volumes. A special debt of thanks is owed to Mr J. Robbie, who allowed the author free access to his files relating to the Deeside Railway Preservation Committee.

All authors are to some extent beholden to those who have touched on their subject previously and it is a pleasure to acknowledge the help gained in the early stages of writing from the histories of the Great North of Scotland Railway by Sir C. M. Barclay-Harvey and H. A. Vallance. A great deal of useful information was also obtained from the publications of the Great North of Scotland Railway Association. The journey logs in Appendix (8) have been adapted by the author from records kept by Sir C. M. Barclay-Harvey. All of the quotations relating to the period before 1900, and for which no source is given, are from the *Aberdeen Journal*.

Many people have helped by supplying photographs, and these are acknowledged separately. Most of the photographic and copying work for the book was carried out by Microfilm Records (Aberdeen) Limited. The original—rather patchwork—manuscript has been efficiently converted into typescript by Mrs Christine Black. Finally, to all those not mentioned above who have in any way contributed to the preparation of this work, the author offers his heartfelt thanks.

The Illustrations

Ian Allan Ltd, 42; Sir C. M. Barclay-Harvey, 1, 15, 24, 26, 31, 33, 45; P. Mann, 34; L. McKay, 2, 23, 27, 29, 46; A. Thomson, 21, 28; Aberdeen Journals, 3, 32, 39, 40; Inspector Hinchcliffe, 18, 19; N. Forrest, 36; British Railways PRPO (Scottish Region), 43, 44; (London Midland Region), 4; J. Taylor, 16; *London Illustrated News*, 30; A. D. Farr, 5, 6, 7, 8, 9, 10, 11, 12, 13, 14, 17, 20, 22, 35, 37, 38, 41.

The pages of the working timetable for the visit of the Czar of Russia are reproduced by courtesy of the BRB Historical Records Office, Edinburgh. The working timetable page for 1965 and the closure notice are reproduced by courtesy of the PRPO, British Railways (Scottish Region). The poem 'Lament' is reprinted by kind permission of Mrs Innes of Learney and Aberdeen Journals Ltd. The map of the line as at the 1923 grouping is reproduced by courtesy of *The Railway Magazine*. The station layout diagrams are based on the ordnance survey 25,000 series, editions of 1900-01, and were drawn, as were the crest and seal of the Deeside and Aboyne & Braemar Railways, by Mrs Sidney Edwards.

The coloured frontispiece was painted especially for this work by Charles Adams.

Bibliography

Aberdeen Journal
Aberdeen Herald
Daily Free Press
Aberdeen Press & Journal
Aberdeen Evening Express
Deeside Railway Co directors' minutes and Traffic & Finance Committee minutes
Aboyne & Braemar Railway Co directors' minutes
Great North of Scotland Railway Co directors' minutes
Working and public timetables of the Deeside Railway Co, GNS, LNE and BR
GNS rule book, 1867
Bills and Acts of Parliament concerning the Deeside Railway Co, Aboyne & Braemar Railway Co, and the GNS, and the grouping Act of 1922 and Transport Acts of 1947 and 1961
A History of the Great North of Scotland Railway, Sir Malcolm Barclay-Harvey (Loco Pub Co 2nd Edn)
The Great North of Scotland Railway, H. A. Vallance (David & Charles, 1965)
GNSR *Locomotive Notes*, E. C. Craven
Locomotives of the Great North of Scotland Railway, M. C. V. Allchin (Railway Hobbies Ltd, 1950)
Great North of Scotland Railway (Stephenson Locomotive Society, 1954)
Great North Review (GNSRA, Aberdeen)
GNSRA Supplements (GNSRA, Aberdeen)
The Railway Magazine
The LNER *Magazine*
Railway World
The Deeside Field
The Deeside Railway Preservation Committee minutes and correspondence. Reports Nos 1 and 2 by Kinord Associates

Index

Illustrations are indicated by heavy type